Traveling with the Life-Giver

A Spiritual Journey Through Recovery From Abuse

CAROL ROMEO

Copyright © 2022 by Carol Romeo.

ISBN 978-1-64133-896-7 (softcover)
ISBN 978-1-64133-897-4 (ebook)

All rights reserved. No part of this book may be reproduced or transmitted in any form or by any means, electronic or mechanical, including photocopying, recording, or by any information storage and retrieval system without express written permission from the author, except in the case of brief quotations embodied in critical reviews and certain other noncommercial uses permitted by copyright law.

Unless otherwise noted, scripture quotations are taken from the New King James Version. Copyright © 1982 by Thomas Nelson, Inc. Used by permission. All rights reserved.

Scripture quotations marked NLT are from the Holy Bible, New Living Translation. Copyright © 1996 by Tyndale House Publishers, Inc. Used by permission. All rights reserved.

Scripture quotations marked NIV are from the Holy Bible, New International Version. Copyright © 1973, 1978, 1984, International Bible Society. Used by permission.

Scripture quotations marked AMPLIFIED are from the Amplified Bible. Old Testament copyright © 1965, 1987 by the Zondervan Corporation. The Amplified New Testament copyright © 1954, 1958, 1987 by the Lockman Foundation. Used by permission.

Printed in the United States of America.

Brilliant Books Literary
137 Forest Park Lane Thomasville
North Carolina 27360 USA

ENDORSEMENTS

When a person is trapped in despair sometimes it seems impossible to take even the first step to recovery and restoration. Through this book you will be inspired to take that first step toward health, and you will be filled with hope as you see that you are never truly alone. The Life-Giver is always near even in the darkest of times; He accepts you and leads you to wholeness as you learn to trust Him.

David Richardson, Dean
Wagner Leadership Institute Pasadena

This book is full of hope but it doesn't deny pain. Reading it is like having a mentor guiding one through the healing process while safely encountering the Life-Giver. Traveling with the Life-Giver is a significant resource for anyone in individual or group therapy. I will recommend it to my clients and to other therapists.

Lloyd Hamner, M.Div., M.A., LMFT
Director of California Christian Counseling Center,
Van Nuys, CA

Carol took the abuse and brokenness from her own life—along with her professional expertise from many years of working in this field—and put them into an allegory illuminating a healing path for the wounded. I highly recommend this book for people who have been the victim of any type of abuse—and for the professionals who work with them. This is a unique and powerful book.

Karin Olson, MSW, ASW

There is hope beyond your abuse! This book will help you through your dark valley of despair until you can receive for yourself Life-Giver's offer of light and the promise of life. Enjoy!

Alyson Andrasik, MFT

This book validated my experience and explained my struggle as a survivor. I found the Life-Giver to be a wonderful comforter and guide. He gives me the courage to press through the difficult process of gaining His promises for my life.

Rebecca, Abuse Survivor

DEDICATION

I dedicate this book to the many men and women whom I have had the privilege of assisting on their journey through recovery. Your courage and diligence inspires me. Thank you for what you have given to me in this process. May Jesus Christ, our Life-Giver, continue to bless you with everything you need to complete your travel into renewed health.

CONTENTS

Introduction ix

Chapter One Leaving the Kingdom 1
   Pathway To Your Healing 7

Chapter Two Entering the Valley of Despair 11
   Pathway To Your Healing 17

Chapter Three Opposing Forces 20
   Pathway To Your Healing 27

Chapter Four A Darkened Abode 30
   Pathway To Your Healing 38

Chapter Five A Turned Heart 42
   Pathway To Your Healing 50

Chapter Six A Way of Escape 54
   Pathway To Your Healing 60

Chapter Seven Walking In The Light 64
   Pathway To Your Healing 69

Chapter Eight The Promise of Life 72
   Pathway To Your Healing 80

Appendix 83

INTRODUCTION

If you are an individual who has experienced abuse, whether it be verbal, physical, emotional, sexual or spiritual, you know that the pathway to peace and wholeness is difficult. All forms of abuse impact our body, soul (emotions, intellect and will) and spirit. It is our whole being that can be damaged and our whole being that requires healing. Where do we turn to find restoration?

In *Traveling with the Life-Giver* I have presented the healing journey from a strong spiritual perspective; nevertheless, I have also sought to demonstrate our psychological, physical and relational struggles in the recovery process. As I continue to counsel those who have suffered abuse, I recognize that we cannot travel this healing journey alone. Although I may not be able to personally visit with you in my counseling office, *Traveling with the Life-Giver* is my attempt to impart to you the wisdom, vision, courage and faith that I have received from our wonderful Life-Giver, Jesus Christ. Further, it is my desire that this writing will guide you on a path where you will personally experience Jesus Christ, through the presence of His Spirit, journeying there beside you.

Pain is isolating. It can cause us to rivet our attention on it and away from others who can help. Often our pain cuts us off from God. How does this happen? Shame, a by-product of all forms of abuse, contributes to our isolation by sending the message to us that we are "damaged goods." We come to believe that we are too damaged to receive God's love. As a result we tend to withdraw from God, the very One who can bring us to health.

Traveling with the Life-Giver depicts the difficult journey through recovery into health and into a right relationship with God. I have chosen to write this as an allegorical story even though the dream, vision and other parts of it were prophetically revealed to me by the Holy Spirit. The Holy Spirit is a vital agent of healing. He may not visit you in a vision or dream; though I encourage you to look and listen for Him. Jesus has sent Him to be your guide and reveal truth to you that leads to healing.

At the end of each chapter is a section entitled "Pathway to Your Healing." It includes helpful observations about the story and insightful questions designed to engender self-reflection as part of your healing process. In my work as a therapist, I have discovered that the more engaged an individual is with their process, the greater the healing. Therefore, I would encourage you to commit to working through the exercises in "Pathway to Your Healing" in your individual or group study.

Whether you have just started your journey toward recovery—or you have been on the pathway to recovery for a while—I would be privileged if you decide to travel with me. It is my hope that through these pages you will:

- Come to know the love of Life-Giver as He reaches into your heart
- Be refreshed and strengthened by the Spirit as He walks by your side
- Step into the healing river of God as it flows from heaven to you
- Become a *healed* healer

May our Lord Jesus bless and heal you as you journey with Him.

A fellow traveler, *Carol Romeo*

Chapter One

LEAVING THE KINGDOM

You know my reproach, my shame, and my dishonor; my adversaries are all before You. Reproach has broken my heart, and I am full of heaviness; I looked for someone to take pity, but there was none; and for comforters, but I found none... Let Your salvation, O God, set me up on high... And you who seek God, your hearts shall live (Psalm 69:19, 20, 29, 32).

Embittered tears dampened Forsaken's face as she scrambled down the treacherous path that led into the blackened forest and away from her beloved Life-Giver's home. In the midst of her uncontrolled outburst at Life-Giver and rash exit, she had forgotten how desolate this forest had become since Enemy King had captured it. Peering into the dark and tangled underbrush ahead of her, Forsaken's uneasiness grew. Breathless from her hasty flight and mismanaged anger, she pulled, swatted and kicked at the twigs and branches that camouflaged her path. Her anger drove her here, but the deeper into the forest she traveled, the more she longed for the not-too-distant security she had experienced while living with Life-Giver. Forsaken sighed deeply. The pain in her heart reminded her that this place is never where she intended to be.

As she looked inward at the darkened condition of her soul, she was stunned. The deep love she had experienced while living with Life-Giver had been replaced with the sad ache of isolation. Her heart chastened her, "Why did you leave the One who made you feel so loved and cherished?"

She paused in the path. Her heart grew heavier as she probed for an answer, "Exactly, why did I leave Life-Giver's home?" But the only response came from the distant silent ache within.

Grasping her sleeve with her hand, she attempted to dry the tears that were now chilling her face. The frigid night air was quickly penetrating her internal being exaggerating the coldness she already experienced without the presence of Life-Giver. She folded her arms tightly against her body to contain the shivering as the pain of isolation shot through her body.

"Betrayal—that was it. Yes, I left because I felt so betrayed by Life-Giver."

Forsaken recalled the events leading up to this moment. She remembered her mother's death and her father's angry tirades and final abandonment of her. In her distress, Life-Giver had taken her into His home and raised her as His child. Although His action did not erase all of her pain, she felt protected and cared for by Him. Those feelings of protection ended, however, the day a stranger named Abuse broke into the home and assaulted her. The pain of violation became mixed with disturbing thoughts over her protector's betrayal.

"Where was He when I needed Him the most?" she questioned. "It doesn't make sense. Is He my friend or not? If He loved me like He said He did, how could He stand idly by while Abuse was attacking me?"

"How could you? I pledged my life to you. I trusted you. I'll never trust you again," she screamed at Life-Giver the day she decided to leave His home.

Her decision to leave was not completely her own, however. Unbeknownst to Forsaken, Enemy King had sent some of his army to deceive her and further *his* plans for her life. He sent Pain and Doubt shortly after the attack from Abuse to persuade Forsaken to depart from Life-Giver.

"Look at the hellish thing that happened to you, Forsaken. Where is your Life-Giver now?" they had jeered.

Pain had reached inside his arsenal and pulled out a slender spear that he slid unobtrusively into Forsaken's heart releasing the poisonous lie concerning Life-Giver's unfaithfulness.

Forsaken had not yet recognized the gruesome fact that Pain and Doubt and some other devilish companions would accompany her through most of her travels. The Spirit of Life-Giver would always be close by, although her enemies would do their best to hide that truth from her. Their wicked plan was executed well. As Forsaken surrendered to their deceptive influence, she became increasingly blinded to the truth of Life-Giver's faithfulness. And, as she traveled on, the farther she got from Life-Giver, the more she agreed with her enemy, "Life-Giver did betray me!"

Forsaken's darkened heart, content with the falsehoods placed there by the enemy, propelled her dangerously deeper into the territory of Enemy King. As she fumbled along the rugged passage, Forsaken had no idea what destruction awaited her in the darkness ahead. She was quickly losing power over the hidden regions of her mind and the enemy would use that against her.

Still, the Spirit sought to persuade her to return and at every clearing in the path He urged her, "Come this way, Cherished."

At the Spirit's urging, she paused and reflected, "I do *so* love that name, Cherished, the name Life-Giver gave to me."

Pain and Doubt stood poised and ready to intercept that thought, but then realized it wasn't necessary.

Without skipping a beat, Forsaken continued, "Yes, I did love that name, but I can no longer believe it is true of me."

Doubt could not contain himself any longer, so he leaned over and in a scoffing tone that only he could produce, announced to her, "Forsaaaken, your name is Forsaaaken and don't you forget it!"

It was Doubt who had whispered that new name, *Forsaken*, into Cherished's ears the day she left Life-Giver's kingdom. She was not especially fond of that name, but it seemed to suit her at the time, and so she kept it. The enemy's tactics were crafty. As Cherished embraced and rehearsed her new name, Forsaken, she could no longer see herself as Life-Giver saw her and she failed to respond to His calling.

As she groped her way through the mass of thickening brushwood, the increasing darkness threatened her every step. Forsaken wondered, "Will I ever discover a path out of this darkened place? Will I experience joy again? Where are my inner songs that used to lighten my steps?" She tread heavily now, for her once-joyous songs had become silent, desperate cries for the night itself to envelop her. Anxiety crept over her and she almost ran back to her beloved's side when Doubt snatched her arm.

"Remember your *beloved's betrayal*," he bullied.

This time his lies penetrated more easily as Forsaken's blindness to the truth had increased. She nodded her agreement to her enemy as she disappeared into the rough terrain leading away from the Kingdom of Life-Giver.

The darkness of the shrouded path continued to deepen into her soul. Forsaken entered a small clearing and stared upward, straining to detect some light from either the moon or stars. But the sky was void and empty of any radiance that could guide her. She would soon discover that inside the enemy territory there is often a concealing of the light that is present in the Kingdom of Life-Giver. Forsaken was not eager to learn any more about this new territory and she sat in the clearing hoping to gain some strength for the rest of the journey.

Forsaken withdrew inwardly as she rested and searched her heart to find a little hope in the midst of her saddened condition. As she dared to breathe a prayer into the night (which was *very* daring in her present state of mind), she thought she felt the breath of Life-Giver. It was just a humble breeze brushing against her stilled soul. And even though she questioned its presence inside the enemy territory, she was grateful for the added strength she was experiencing. Therefore, in spite of the gravelike darkness, she struggled to her feet to resume her pace.

Unaware of her immediate danger, Forsaken stepped into the forbidden war zone. Her enemy, Doubt, who made himself known, positioned himself on her left and the Spirit of Life-Giver, who remained unseen, moved swiftly to her right. At Forsaken's next step, a large fiendish creature assaulted her mind. She had never encountered anything like him before and she was shaken to her core. Trembling, she stumbled and would have fallen had it not been for the unseen Spirit who supported her.

Confused and reeling from the attack, she muttered to the creature, "Who are you?"

He withheld his reply until the Spirit of Life-Giver poked him with His fiery sword.

"Abuse," he blurted out as he glared into her eyes. "I was present here, in your mind, every time you were abused. Not only did I watch, but I also etched those experiences in your memory. Look, they are all here for you to see."

Forsaken gasped and nearly fainted, "Abuse…no. I mustn't look!"

Feeling overwhelmed by the enormity of what he was saying and his aggressive stance towards her, Forsaken nearly lost her senses and bolted towards a more dangerous part of the war zone. Doubt stopped her. His motive was to detain her long enough for Abuse to whisper all her secrets back to her.

Abuse tightened his strangling grip around Forsaken's mind. She felt sickened in her soul as she rehearsed to herself how long and hard she had labored to keep those memories from intruding into her present life. "This isn't fair!" she murmured to herself. "It is bad enough that my abuse actually happened, but when I think of replaying the events, it is just too much!" (Life-Giver had promised to use the knowledge concerning her past to set her free from her present darkness, but she had forgotten that promise.)

Forsaken tried to free herself from the stronghold of Abuse. Her attempt failed miserably, and as she sunk to the ground in defeat, she found herself clutched even more securely by her vicious enemies Doubt and Abuse. Forsaken began to weep. Her heart pounded so wildly she thought she might die. "But then, death might be a sweet reprieve," she thought.

When the Spirit of Life-Giver recognized that she was weakening, He reached into His own heart and, unnoticed by the others, bent low and deposited some of His own vitality into Forsaken's heart. This action went unnoticed by Forsaken as well, although she did recognize that she suddenly felt a little more hopeful and thoughts of death were momentarily abated. The Spirit helped her to her feet and Abuse, recognizing the aid of some unseen force, loosened his hold on her. Forsaken didn't know it yet, but the Spirit of Life-Giver was going to help her find her way through this darkened path, even though the enemy would try and hinder her efforts.

Much to Abuse's dismay, Forsaken regained her footing along the desolate pathway. Without Abuse's hold on her mind, she was able to lift her head a bit and she could now perceive shadows of her surroundings. The silhouettes of her dreaded companions did not seem as threatening as before when the darkness had completely consumed her thinking.

In fact, Forsaken began to have flashbacks of the happy times when she would run with her beloved Life-Giver through the sun-bathed fields, the warm gentle breezes fluffing her hair. She remembered the laughter she loved sharing with Him. Her senses were filled with the sweet fragrances lifted from the flowering hillside and the perfume rising from the presence of her beloved. For a moment her senses lifted her above her detestable condition and her soul and spirit were refreshed.

The path widened a bit and Forsaken was thankful that she did not have to give as much attention to clearing the brush ahead of her. As the trees opened a pathway before her, she noticed something unusual—a brilliant light. "What is that strange light?" she cried, delighted that she could see more clearly. But, she was mostly delighted with the alluring presence the light exuded as it seeped through the trees, surrounded her body and excited her soul.

"It reminds me of the way Life-Giver's loving presence invited and sheltered my heart," she commented to herself.

Forsaken followed the light beam as she made her way around curves, inclines and dips in the path.

"It seems to be guiding my steps," she mused as her thoughts turned to Life-Giver and the way He had lovingly guided her through their many travels together.

"I wish you were here," she whispered, not recognizing that His Spirit was already at her side.

Finally, the path ended abruptly at the rim of a steep embankment that emptied into the Valley of Despair. Forsaken's focus, however, was drawn to the other side of the canyon and she lifted her head to see where the source of the light was coming from. The light flittered its way into her eyes and captured her attention. Forsaken's awareness of her dismal surroundings slipped away as she viewed this lush land on the other side of the valley.

As she did so, the Spirit of Life-Giver spoke into her heart, "This is where I'm taking you. Don't be afraid."

She wept silently, awed by this heavenly sight.

She contemplated, "Do I dare believe? I have been disappointed so many times before. My heart could not withstand yet another disappointment, especially one this big."

Yet, she could not deny it. There it was—visible to her eyes. She could see herself freely dancing in the greenest, grandest meadow she had ever imagined. The tattered and stained garment she usually wore was replaced with a pure white gown that glowed in the warm sunlight with the same sparkle she noticed glistening on her face. As she observed herself twirling about she commented, "I look so beautiful and *so* happy!"

The Spirit asked, "Will you come with Me?"

She replied, "Yes, take me there!"

Forsaken was so enamored by the light, she became largely unaware that the journey to that place of wholeness was through the Valley of Despair.

Pathway **TO YOUR HEALING**

1. All kinds of abuse have one thing in common: they all test our internal resources. Cherished's internal resources were tested during her encounter with Abuse. Since she already knew Life-Giver, she felt unprotected and therefore abandoned by Life-Giver. She had reached an end of her internal resources. However, instead of remaining and reaching out for help, she ran. She believed the lies of her enemy that Life-Giver was not there for her.

    a. In what ways have your internal resources been tried? What does your present or past abuse look like? Try not to minimize your own abuse or compare it with someone else's experience. Abuse more or less is all the same. It *all* exhausts our emotional strengths.

b. What is your relationship with Jesus Christ (Life-Giver) like? Cherished projected her parental relationship (abandoning) onto Life-Giver. How do you see Him?
c. Satan and his forces use our weak places against us and can plant lies in our minds to stop the plans of God. Can you recognize some of the lies he uses with you?

2. Anger is a common response to abuse and neglect. It is an emotion that can warn us that someone has harmed us. It becomes destructive, however, when we allow it to turn into bitterness or rage against the abuser, God, or ourselves. We may "act out" in behaviors that are unhealthy. One way that Forsaken acted out was retreating from Life-Giver and His home. This resulted in her refusal to receive His help, comfort and ultimately His truth. It was her angry heart that also made the lies of the enemy more appealing.

   a. Where are you on an anger scale of 0–10? Who are you angry at?
   b. How are you acting out your bitterness or rage?
   c. Are you open to receiving help, comfort or truth from Jesus?

3. This story elaborates on the interaction between three different forces: Life-Giver (Jesus Christ), Enemy King and his army (Satan and his demonic forces) and Forsaken's choices (human will and choice). Although Forsaken already knew Life-Giver (she lived with Him), she made a decision to come out from under His covering (blessing and protection) and walk a path He had not designed for her. This choice led her into a place where her heart was darkened to Life-Giver's love and her mind was darkened to the truth of His Word. Cherished would eventually forsake her own name and embrace a name the enemy gave her, Forsaken, whereby rejecting Life-Giver's vision and plan for her life.

   a. Can you recognize the three different forces at work in your life? We can strengthen the power of Jesus Christ in our lives as we make choices that line up with His truth. What choices are you making?

b. Do you see yourself as Christ sees you today or the enemy? What truth about your life can you embrace today?

c. What is the vision Christ has given you concerning your life? Are you following that vision or embracing the name the enemy has given you?

4. A psychological occurrence that is common to most abuse survivors is something called flashbacks: fragments of the traumatic event intruding on the mind, body or emotions. The event is replayed: (1) in the mind as thoughts or pictures, (2) in the body as specific body memories from the event, and (3) in the emotions as the accompanying feelings.

   Flashbacks can come all at once, or they can come in bits and pieces. If we can process the abusive event with all its different components and invite Jesus to heal our wounds, we will discover that our recovery is greatly benefited. As we do this, we might discover (as did Forsaken) that the enemy wants to stir up the memories to cause fear and keep us in bondage to the pain. That is not Jesus' intent. When He uncovers something, it is for our healing.

   a. What has been your experience (in past and present) with flashbacks?

   b. Have you worked diligently, as Forsaken did, to hide those abuse memories deep inside yourself? How much fear do you have concerning the retrieval of the memories?

   c. Can you allow the Spirit to access the memories to bring healing?

5. The Spirit (Holy Spirit) will always travel with us, even in the darkest of times. He is there to direct us (with His light), to strengthen us with His power (He deposited His own vitality into Forsaken's heart) and to uncover truth to us concerning

the love of Jesus. But, His effectiveness is limited at times by the choices that we make.

a. What choices are you making today concerning the Spirit's leading? Where is He leading you? Can you say "yes?"
b. Will you dare to breathe a prayer to the Lord in the midst of your darkness? He is faithful to meet you there.
c. Can you open yourself to the vision or hope the Holy Spirit has to give you?

Chapter Two

ENTERING THE VALLEY OF DESPAIR

But when I looked for good, evil came to me; and when I waited for light, then came darkness. My heart is in turmoil and cannot rest; days of affliction confront me. I go about mourning, but not in the sun; I stand in the assembly and cry out for help... My harp is turned to mourning, and my flute to the voice of those who weep" (Job 30:26–28, 31).

The lovely vision of dancing in the green sunlit meadow remained in Forsaken's heart and mind for quite a while. In fact, she was still thinking about it when Doubt, angered by her lofty contemplations, tripped her and she fell headlong down the perilous mountainside leading into the Valley of Despair.

"Hah! You think you can stay in your fanciful place? You are wrong, Ms Forsaken!" he screeched proudly.

As she rapidly plummeted down, Abuse once again attacked her mind. This time, however, he unleashed a torrent of loathsome memories over which she had no power. Before this, Forsaken always had some control over the memories, but the fall overwhelmed her senses and she could not manage one complete thought on her own. Pain, also, advanced on her and hurled venomous spears into her heart and body as he helped propel her downward. He had gained access to her through

Abuse; nevertheless, Despair, the ruler of this valley, would grant him even greater control.

Forsaken's plunge came to an abrupt end as she smashed into the valley floor. She shook her head and attempted to regain her sanity, but her tragic memories continued to fully impact her. Contorted in her thinking, she spouted, "Why did I survive this fall? Is there no way to end my pain and suffering?"

With thoughts of the land across the valley yielding to the blackness that invaded her mind, Forsaken lay motionless for a considerable time until the Spirit of Life-Giver, her unseen advocate, distanced Pain and Abuse from her body. He lingered about her longing to comfort her, but He recognized that in her disillusionment she would refuse Him. The voice of the enemy was very clear now: "You'll never be the same again, Forsaken. Look at your demented condition."

She raised her head to look around.

"He is right," she declared inwardly. "The deep darkness in this valley can't even hide my darkened soul."

"Life-Giver, I thought You were taking me to the green meadow. I don't understand. You said You'd be with me, but I can't see You. Where are You? How will I make it through? I can't do it without You," she pleaded.

Greatly moved by her petition for help, the Spirit reached down and lifted her to her feet. Abuse was still stammering his lies, though now Forsaken could hear the subtle voice of the Spirit saying, "I am here." His reassurance wasn't enough to excite renewed faith in her heart, but it was enough to strengthen her resolve to continue the journey.

As Pain, Doubt and Abuse became aware of her newly-found resolve, they became determined to stick even more closely to her. "One of us must be at her side at all times," Pain asserted. "I don't know where she is getting her aid from, but I am sure that together we can deter it."

If they had known it was the Spirit of Life-Giver, they may not have planned such a bold action. Their power was no match for Life-Giver and they knew it. However, they also knew that inside the Valley of Despair, His power was largely forgotten by the human dwellers.

Imprisoned by a curtain of darkness that had menacingly spread its borders over the somber valley, Forsaken labored along the shadowed path with her enemies still at her side. This valley belonged to Enemy King and his oppressive presence was quite evident. She knew it must be day; nevertheless, she was disheartened to see only a tiny glimmer of light poking through the sinister-looking clouds that had formed during the night. She had hoped that the arrival of daylight would offer clues as to her whereabouts because she had lost all sense of direction during the fall.

Forsaken looked down for a moment and suddenly realized something was missing. She blurted, "My bag, I lost my bag! I must have dropped it when I fell. What will I do without it?" Forsaken's anxiety heightened. She recognized her bag contained items essential to her survival—her coat, blanket and the food Life-Giver had given her when she left His home.

Distraught, Forsaken started to hurry back to where she thought she had landed after her fall. The Spirit, eager to help, rushed ahead of her, retrieved her bag and placed it on a large rock close to the place where she had fallen. Forsaken wound her way back to the foot of the mountain, and when she got there she dropped to her knees and began to feverishly search the area.

Doubt, of course, was right next to her speaking into her ear, "You'll never find it. You might as well give up. Why bother hoping and sadden yourself even further?"

When those remarks did not deter her from her task, he added, "You know you don't deserve anything good. That is why you left the Kingdom of Life-Giver. You weren't good enough!"

At that last remark, Forsaken began to cry. "Maybe I am right to doubt," she conceded. "It is too scary to believe for the good. Look at my scars. They prove it. I am bad. Who am I to search for something good?"

The Spirit, however, was close by. He gently turned her head in the direction of the bag and illuminated it just enough for her to notice it. She quickly lunged at it as if, not seized, it immediately would vanish.

Shaking from both the expected dreaded loss *and* the excitement of her newfound treasure, Forsaken strained at the frozen clasp that secured the bag. When she finally got it unfastened, she opened the bag energetically and peered inside. She yanked out her favorite red-hooded, fur lined coat from the sack. Then she pulled out her blanket that she never ever slept without. And she uncovered the meal that Life-Giver had left for her. She was delighted to find the bread that she loved so much. (It was always fresh because it was baked every day at Life-Giver's home.) She was equally pleased to find a bottle of grape juice. (It was squeezed daily from the extraordinary grape vines in His garden.)

"But wait, what is this at the very bottom?" she asked herself as she stuck her hand deep into the bag. "I... I didn't pack anything else," she stammered out loud.

"Wow, it's a leather pouch with something in it... Oh no, it can't be! This is Life-Giver's Promise Book! Why would He send that with *me*, especially after I told Him I didn't believe any of His promises anymore?"

Despite what had transpired, she was warmed by her memory of the times she and Life-Giver would visit together. Every night, she would sit ever so close to Life-Giver as He read her favorite stories from His favorite book to her.

"I used to love hearing His promises," she sighed. "They really did change my heart."

The fondness in her voice sickened Abuse and Doubt who became alarmed and angry at Life-Giver. "How dare He sneak by us and deposit His *precious* book into Forsaken's bag!" they hissed.

They were personally very aware of how dangerous Life-Giver's promises are to their kingdom. Quietly, they talked back and forth to one another: "How can we get her to throw this Promise Book away? Let's distract her and barrage her mind with bad memories of her abuse," they conspired. "We won't let up until she tosses the book!"

The thoughts and images Abuse and Doubt planted in her mind swam so fast through Forsaken's brain that she was set off balance. Without even thinking about it, she grabbed the Promise Book and clasped it to her chest. This action further angered Doubt and Abuse.

"I thought she would toss the book away, just as she did when we first incited her in Life-Giver's home. I remember. She had vowed then never to read the Promise Book again," snarled Abuse.

Together, Doubt and Abuse demanded of Enemy King who was watching close by, "What is she doing, clutching that book to her heart?" Enemy King remained silent.

Forsaken's enemies stood confused and frozen at her side while the Spirit leaned in and whispered to her, "These promises will renew your mind."

Forsaken shamefully lowered her head and softened her voice as she acknowledged, "I am not yet willing to believe that."

The Spirit, however, was not convinced that Forsaken's heart was as deadened to Life-Giver's words as she assessed. "I want to show her the faith I know her heart is capable of," He suggested to Life-Giver. In unison, they devised a plan.

The Spirit moved closer to Forsaken, secretly removed a piece of bread from her bag and placed it in her hand. Forsaken looked at the bread and without forethought began eating it. As she did, the Spirit reminded her of these words from Life-Giver, "I am *the bread*. I am *the way.*"

With that, she began to wonder, "What if it is true? Maybe Life-Giver *can* show me another way out of this valley!"

Doubt could not believe his ears. "How did her mind jump there?"

Enraged and confused about what action to take, he enlisted the help of Pain who had been positioned close by. Pain knew exactly what to do to send her back into the unbelief. He reached for his poisonous spear and once again he thrust it into her heart.

"Aaaaaaaah!" Forsaken screeched in horror.

But Pain didn't stop there. He sent another thrust into her mind, unleashing the rest of the deluge of terror there. Trembling, Forsaken fell to the ground. Thoughts erupted in her mind, "How was I so stupid to think there was another way? No one can help ease this tragic pain in my heart, not even Life-Giver."

As Forsaken sat crumbled on the valley floor, she glanced up the valley wall from where she had fallen earlier. Now there was no light at the top, not even a little bit.

She grumbled to herself, "There is no other way for me."

Convinced once more that the path through the Valley of Despair was her only choice, Forsaken wrestled to her feet, gathered up her scant belongings and readied herself the best she could for her solitary journey. It didn't take her long to become acutely aware of how desolate this place really was. There seemed to be no evidence of life here at all. No small animals scurried through the brush. No lizards slinked across the footpath.

"I haven't seen any birds flying through this awful, thick haze. No one is out here but me," she moaned within herself.

An eerie but familiar feeling swept over her. She was reluctant to announce, "I know that presence well. It is Death."

Forsaken began thinking about it. A desire to die had continually polluted her mind ever since the attack from Abuse. Forsaken hated to admit that sometimes Death was her only source of comfort when she felt stripped and alone. Even though she was aware that she probably would not take his pathway of escape, she was strangely soothed by his fatal promises and oddly pleased that he was with her now.

By now, Forsaken was aimlessly meandering down the path. Failing to notice a sudden drop before her, she slipped and slid down a small incline. She grabbed Death's arm to try and regain her footing. He was more than willing to oblige her, as this furthered his opportunity to influence her to accept his way.

This was very distressing to the Spirit who attempted to gain her attention. "Look here, I am with you," He coaxed. But Forsaken couldn't hear Him since she had given herself more fully to Death.

Even with the enemy's help, however, she found that the path was becoming more difficult to travel. It was fiercely irregular and strewn with rocks of all sizes. In fact, on several occasions, she had to grip Death's arm even more tightly to steady herself. Pain secured her other arm and Doubt and Abuse walked tightly beside them. Together, they rehearsed her sad plight over and over again.

"You are so stupid to think that Life-Giver will save you," breathed Doubt. "He can't love you. Look at how pitiful you are."

"It hurts too much to keep going," snarled Pain.

"Remember those awful acts..." said Abuse with unusual smugness.

Death mocked, "Why don't you just stop trying. You want to die anyway."

In desperation, Forsaken tried drowning out their voices by repeating Life-Giver's promises: *"I am loved by Life-Giver. He is the way. He gives me life. He does want the best for me."* Nevertheless, her confusion was too great and she had become too weak. There were times when her enemies' voices became so deafening that she risked losing her balance and released her traveling companions to cover her ears. Finally, half crazed, she lunged her body forward to the ground and shook as violent cries poured from her inner being.

She protested, "What has happened to my life? What is this pain that has carved out my soul? Look at my state, Life-Giver. Do you care? I am neither dead nor alive. What is to become of me?"

She hesitated. Pain stabbed her heart once again and toughened it against her beloved Life-Giver.

She blurted, "Life-Giver, I never want to see You again."

Forsaken wept quietly while her enemies sent a wave of remorse over her.

Their lies pierced her soul: "You've done it this time. You will get exactly what you asked for. You will never see Him again."

Pathway **TO YOUR HEALING**

1. When we are abused, the lie that the enemy likes to feed us is, "I'm bad and therefore undeserving of anything good." If Satan can get us to believe that lie, we will not hope and we will not reach out to God for anything good. Many times, as abuse survivors, we blame ourselves because it is the least threatening thing to do. If we continue to do this, it becomes easy to enter into self-defeating and self-destructive behaviors.

    a. Have you ever thought: "I'm bad and therefore undeserving of anything good"? Have you ever believed that lie about yourself?
    b. What are the results of believing the lie in your thoughts, emotions, spirit and behavior?
    c. What is the truth?

2. Many times, especially if our painful journey is long, we can fall into hopelessness or despair. In that state, it becomes easier to toss aside those things that we need for our spiritual or emotional survival.

    Forsaken had discarded her bag during her fall into despair (Valley of Despair). Inside the bag were the essentials she needed to survive her journey. The bread and grape juice in her bag represents Christ. The displaced blanket images the comfort of the Spirit. And her coat corresponds to the covering or protection of Jesus.

    a.   Are you presently or have you been in a state of despair? What has your despair been like?
    b.   What are the essentials that you have tossed aside in your despair?
    c.   What do you want to retrieve? The Spirit is ready to help you. The Spirit showed Forsaken where her bag was, even though she was disheartened and disillusioned.

3. The Life-Giver included His Promise Book (the Bible) in her bag because He knew that His promises were the weapons that would cut through the enemy's lies and help Forsaken to find a way through the darkness. His promises would also remind her that He was with her and would never leave. Sadly, Forsaken discarded the Promise Book for a season until she could gain enough confidence that the promises were indeed truth.

    a.   How has your abuse or descent into despair affected your belief in the Word of God?
    b.   What promises are difficult for you to believe and apply?
    c.   The Spirit wants to renew your mind with His promises. What scriptures can you rehearse?

4. Pain is a part of every abuse survivor's journey. With each kind of abuse (spiritual, physical, emotional or sexual), there comes a wounding to the soul. Sometimes we seek to manage it through our defenses of denial, repression or dissociation. However, eventually these defenses will wear down or abruptly malfunction due to a life crisis or internal stress. Forsaken's pain was magnified by her belief that Life-Giver had deserted her. She ran away from Him and others who could aid her in her pain. In actuality, this led to an increase in pain.

Jesus' motives are to uncover your wounds to *heal* them. Yes, it is a painful journey, but you don't have to spiral down alone in your pain. You can reach out to Christ and others.

    a. What are some of the ways that you have tried to manage your pain? Do you experience fear when you think about revisiting the pain?
    b. In what way (s) has the enemy used your pain against you? Have you removed yourself from Christ or others who can comfort, strengthen or heal you?
    c. Can you believe (even a little) that there is another way out of the pain? Can you allow Jesus into your wounds to heal you?

5. In spite of our efforts to manage our pain or stay connected to God in the process, there are times when the trial has become too long and our internal resources have worn down. The lies from the enemy have more power over us when we are in that state because of our inability to fight.

    You may be like Forsaken and think that Jesus has forsaken you. Or you may feel that the darkness that has come with your depression has swallowed you up. You may have thoughts of suicide, or you may simply desire a "way out." That is when you need someone else.

    a. Are you presently in a depression? Do you feel like you are at the end of your resources? Please let someone know.
    b. Do you have thoughts of suicide or a plan of suicide? If you answered "yes," please let someone know.
    c. Jesus has a better plan for your life, even though you may not be able to see that plan now. Ask Jesus to help you reach out to Him and to others. As you do, you will begin to see that you are not alone in your pain. And you will begin to experience hope that you can complete your journey through your own wilderness with good companions at your side.

Chapter Three

OPPOSING FORCES

Then I saw heaven opened, and a white horse was standing there. Its rider was named Faithful and True, for he judges fairly and wages a righteous war. His eyes were like flames of fire, and on his head were many crowns. A name was written on him that no one understood except himself. He wore a robe dipped in blood, and his title was the Word of God (Revelation 19:11, 13, NLT).

The Spirit of Life-Giver moved in close to Forsaken now and knelt beside her on the ground where she lay sobbing. Resting His hand on her head, He quieted her mind. Forsaken's weeping began to subside. Exhausted from her ordeal and free from the haunting memories, Forsaken yielded to sleep.

"I so desire to bring comfort to Forsaken," the Spirit said to Himself.

He left her side just for a moment to retrieve her bag from the place she had tossed it. Returning, the Spirit pulled out her red jacket and gently covered her. He also searched out her blanket, rolled it up and placed it firmly under her head, taking great care not to wake her. "I will guard her through her sleep," the Spirit said as He glared menacingly at her enemies who stood a distance away.

The Spirit opened the Promise Book to His favorite place and began to read aloud. At the same time, He whispered a thought to Life-Giver,

"I know the power hidden in Your promises; let Your truth cleanse her mind."

Knowing that the enemy hates truth, the Spirit declared boldly to Enemy King, "This truth will pierce your heart like a sword."

The Spirit continued to read from the Promise Book. He blessed the sleeping Forsaken with these words: "And you shall know the truth, and the truth shall make you free" (John 8:32). Regardless of the fact that Forsaken had recently rejected Life-Giver and His promises, the Spirit knew Life-Giver would keep His promises to her. While Forsaken slept, hidden from her enemies, Life-Giver visited her in a dream.

He came to her from out of the sky, riding on a majestic white horse. The horse appeared strong and muscular, and it was stunningly beautiful. Forsaken lifted her hand to stroke its dazzling white coat. She could not remove her gaze.

"I have never seen anything so grand!" she exclaimed.

Just then, from His position on top of the horse, Life-Giver extended His hand to her and asked, "Would you like to ride with Me? There is something I would like to show you."

She stood speechless and amazed. Forsaken had never seen Life-Giver clothed with such radiance. His pure white garment flowed over His body and down past His feet, framing the girth of the huge animal on which He sat.

"Life-Giver, you're so beautiful," she managed to speak.

She reached up, placed her hand in His and fixed her eyes into His penetrating, caring eyes. As He drew her up to His side, His compassionate love was drawing her into His heart. Secured by Life-Giver's arms and supported by the stature of the large horse, she felt safe as they galloped through the expansive sky, the stallion's massive hoofs scattering the clouds as they traveled. Forsaken leaned forward to wrap her arms around the animal's neck and she noticed a golden collar with the word HOPE etched in it.

"What an appropriate name for this powerful friend," she thought.

Then Life-Giver leaned in close to her ear. Pointing to the land below them, He whispered, "This is what I want you to see."

Forsaken glanced down at it, but was bewildered by what she observed, "All I see is land and people in ruin. From fires. Earthquakes. Disease. Famine. Wars. Unruly behavior." She turned inquisitively to Life-Giver expecting an explanation. As He turned towards her, she noticed tears spilling out of His eyes. His tears touched her head and ran down her face.

Grief-stricken, Life-Giver lamented, "This is not the kind of world I created. I intended good and not evil."

With that observation, Life-Giver gently touched the scars on Forsaken's arms and legs left by Abuse. Life-Giver didn't speak anything. He didn't need to. Forsaken saw the pain present in His eyes and she understood: "These wounds and my abuse were not what He had designed for me."

Hope sped off toward the heavenly region. Life-Giver raised His sword and cut the veil that separated the material and the spiritual world. A brilliant light now encompassed them and beckoned them forward into a river that flowed out from the center of the light. Hope galloped through the midst of the river, its waters parting at his advance.

"This water is as clear as crystal. It's odd, though, that just the spray from the river seems to refresh me greatly," she pondered.

Life-Giver now urged, "Forsaken, look around you."

As she lifted her eyes she could see the hordes of hell surrounding them. These creatures were perched on large beasts, and they were brandishing bloody swords and spears.

Their fierce glare towards Forsaken caused her to gasp, "Shall we live?"

Life-Giver said, "Look again!"

This time He expanded her vision so that she could see the brilliant light forming an impenetrable wall between her and the enemy.

"My presence," Life-Giver said, "is able to keep you safely in My kingdom."

As He spoke those words, Forsaken's eyes were further opened and she could see the army of Life-Giver's warring angels who were positioned in the expanse beyond. Their immense stature commanded attention. Forsaken turned to Life-Giver.

"They are very impressive, indeed," she asserted.

Life-Giver elaborated the scene before them. "War in the heavenly realms is an extension of My mercy. Even though you cannot see My mercy with your normal human eyes, it is always active on your behalf."

Almost immediately, Forsaken's senses were overtaken by the thundering roar of hooves hitting the atmosphere like bombs exploding. It was Enemy King's army. With weapons bared they were rushing past Hope towards the land below. The names on their helmets declared their intent: Death, Pain,

Abuse, Hatred, Fear, Sorrow, Hopelessness, Self-hatred, Rebellion, Pride, Loneliness, Despair, and Unworthiness.

As these fiends passed by her, Forsaken became sick in her soul. She recounted, "Each one of these hideous creatures has attacked me and lied to me. They attacked so many times and in so many different ways that I cannot bear to watch this assault also."

In horror and pain, she turned away.

Life-Giver embraced her tightly and whispered His assurance, "It's not over."

Then Forsaken was moved by a strange, but majestic voice that resounded out of heaven. The voice rumbled through her ears and reverberated throughout her tiny earthly being. It was like none she had ever heard. Captivated by the voice, she proposed, "It is a lion's roar, the thunder of rushing water and a trumpet's blast—all merged into one!"

Forsaken peered up toward the direction of the sound as the heavens convulsed in a crescendo and poured out the powerful angelic army that was clad in armor and ready for battle. This powerful unearthly army rode swiftly toward the earthly kingdom on white steeds, also dressed for war. The huge battle-ready horses marched into the river itself, which was now surging through the heavenly gates and gaining momentum as it flowed out to the inhabitants below.

*In the midst of the deafening clamor, Forsaken heard a shout from Life-Giver: "**Life** to those inhabitants of the earthly kingdom, **life** to all those who will get into the river and **life** to those who hear My voice."*

At that proclamation, Forsaken awoke. Disoriented, she sat up and inspected her environment to assess her whereabouts. The dream had so captivated her that she was not sure which world she resided in. As she glanced about, the stark terrain reminded her only too quickly of her journey through this Valley of Despair. Now that the dream had faded and she was back to earth, her task seemed unbearable. Once again, she was impacted by her solitary existence. Chilled to her core, she stood, slipped on her jacket and stuffed her blanket in her bag.

"Hmm, I wonder how my blanket and jacket got out of my bag. Well, I have no time to think about that now. I must try and find shelter."

Nightfall was fast approaching and Forsaken's more serious concerns were focused on discovering a way through this darkened place.

"I'm so scared. I don't want to go on. But I must. I can't stay out here in the open," she reasoned.

A fresh gust of icy wind penetrated her frail body. She shuddered either out of fear or cold; she didn't know which. Forsaken pulled her bag close to her chest to block some of the frosty air. Life-Giver's engaging words, however, still rung in her ears: "***Life*** to those inhabitants of the earthly kingdom, ***life*** to all those who will get into the river and ***life*** to those who hear My voice."

"That is what I want," she thought aloud, "I want life. I want to believe what Life-Giver showed me—that He and the angelic army are fighting for me. Was that just a dream or was it truth? Do I dare…?"

Before Forsaken could finish her question, Doubt exploded into her ear, "You can't believe. That was just a dream, a fantasy. Look around you. This is reality. You are alone. All alone."

Once more, Forsaken attempted to embrace the promise, but it eluded her. She wanted to combat Doubt. Nevertheless, her ability to follow through was weakening as an overwhelming sense of emptiness filled her body.

She forced a response, "Doubt is right. Look at this place. It's barren and I'm alone. Forgotten. Empty."

Emptiness was a feeling Forsaken knew well.

Abuse volunteered, "Remember how you felt, Forsaken, when your father hit you and again, when he left?"

Forsaken grew sick. The emptiness that she had experienced in her gut seemed indelibly etched in her memory. She used to feel it in her gut after she was hit. She felt it again when she was orphaned. And, disturbed at this remembrance, she experienced it again after the raging attack from Abuse and the alleged abandonment from Life-Giver. This last experience was the one that caused Forsaken the most grief and the one that prompted her move from Life-Giver's kingdom.

At present, her emptiness and the belief that Life-Giver had forsaken her would lead her further and further into the darkened chambers of her mind where her most troublesome battle would occur. Pain, Doubt and Abuse took advantage of Forsaken's grief and crowded around her once again. Seeking their own agenda, they entered into a secret and deceptive pact against her: "Let's take her to the darkest part of this valley.

We can seduce her into a place where her soul will no longer cry out for Life-Giver."

"I can make sure that she longs for death and not life," proposed Death, who was hovering nearby. "It's best if I keep my presence hidden to Forsaken until it is time to attack, but I will watch closely and be ready to act when you need me."

Forsaken resumed her journey, although she felt quite dejected from her discourse with Doubt and Abuse. She had hoped they would not be traveling on with her.

"Their power over me is increasing. I can feel it," she ashamedly concluded.

Because she had agreed earlier with Doubt, he saw a new opportunity to aggressively and relentlessly attack her mind. As she walked on, his constant barrage of lies and taunts echoed through her head: "Who do you think you are? You will never amount to anything. In fact, you will never be free from the pain of your past. You will never leave this Valley of Despair. You will die here!"

That was a cue to Death who moved swiftly out of the darkness. He lunged at Forsaken from behind, grabbed the hood of her jacket with his large hand and jerked her back. Fear gripped Forsaken's heart. Nevertheless, she managed to wiggle out of her jacket and free herself from Death's stronghold. Screeching loudly, she sped down the unlit path albeit straight into the arms of a tall stranger.

Instinctively, she began beating wildly on his chest as she ranted, "Get away from me, Death, you can't have me."

She continued her pounding and screeching until the stranger secured her with his strong arms. It took several moments for the stranger to quiet her. Over and over again he kept stating, "I'm not who you think I am. I'm not Death."

Finally Forsaken relaxed, as did the arms of the stranger. She took some long deep breaths before removing herself from his side.

"I'm sorry," Forsaken said. "I just got scared and…"

The stranger interrupted her, "No need to worry. I've survived greater attacks than this. Where are you going?"

"I… I'm traveling through this valley to the mountain on the other side," she stammered.

"Well, I'm the ruler in this region. My name is Despair. Maybe I can help."

Forsaken had heard stories about this ruler and they weren't good. Uneasy about accepting help from him, she delayed her response.

Despair noticed her hesitation. In one steady motion, he bent over and picked up a lantern he had been carrying. "It's awfully dark in this valley at night and a lantern can help. Besides, I know the shortest path across the valley. I'd hate to see you lost."

To himself, Despair screamed, "I've got her now."

It seemed to Forsaken that the riskier undertaking would be traveling at night alone and without light. Despair's offer seemed reasonable enough, but something gnawed at her stomach as she replied, "Well, OK. I will travel with you."

"I'm delighted to hear your invitation," he hissed. Because he feared she might change her mind, he quickly grasped her arm to guide her down the path.

Forsaken shivered.

Despair stopped for a moment. "Do you not have a coat, Miss...?"

Not wanting to give Death credit for his attack and fearful of uncovering his whereabouts (lest it be used against her) Forsaken replied, "I lost my coat back there."

"Here, take my cape, Miss...?" Despair suggested as he unfastened the tie to his cape, swooped it off his shoulders and dropped it onto hers.

Now Death stealthily crept up behind Forsaken and slyly inched the hood over her head. A cool gush of wind swept over her, but Death's tactic went unnoticed. This was the response Death had hoped for. With Forsaken's attention fixed on her dark suitor—Despair—Death would be free to lull her into submission to his plan.

"Miss, can I inquire again what your name is?" Despair questioned.

"Forsaken. My name is Forsaken," she responded with greater resolve than she had earlier.

She was inwardly saddened by her own response. However, she was surprised to discover that acknowledging her name made her traveling companion, Despair, more appealing. Despair extended his hand to her and together they resumed their journey.

Pathway **TO YOUR HEALING**

1. Jesus wants to reveal Himself and His love to you. **You** are why He came to earth and was crucified.

    It is so easy for us earth-bound people to forget the spiritual realm and focus on what we can tangibly see around us. I encourage you to open your spiritual eyes because through the spiritual realm you will find all you need for your difficult journey. Christ, by His Spirit, is the One who travels with you. We cannot hope to find *real life* without *life* in the Spirit! There is a battle between light and dark, good and evil, and God's army is always fighting for us. We, on the other hand, cannot enter into the battle until we can see it. Beloved, open your eyes.

    a. In what ways has Jesus made Himself known to you? What was that experience like?
    b. What do you know about the spiritual world and the battle waged in it?
    c. Can you join the Holy Spirit in the battle against the enemy of your soul?
    d. What are the names of your spiritual enemies? Ask someone to enter into prayer with you against them.

2. In this war between good and evil there are two things we need to remember: (1) God is good and (2) Satan is bad. Jesus did not create your suffering and pain; He wants to take you out of your suffering. Christ comes to bring life and not death. Those messages get all mixed up when we are suffering. The enemy wants to confuse us. If he can make God the bad guy, we won't go to God for help and we won't embrace life.

    a. What is your experience with the message, "God is good and Satan is bad?" Are there places the enemy has confused you?
    b. How are you moving towards life and not death?

    c. What do you think it means to be alert in the Spirit? Are you?

3. Forsaken feared the unknown and so she opened herself to guidance from Despair. (The enemy is always willing to offer us false light.) She had never been through the darkened territory before and she was afraid. Fear can open us up to all kinds of decisions that we may not arrive at otherwise. It is important to remember that Jesus, by His Spirit, is always with us even when we cannot hear or see Him or the territory is new. We can turn fear into faith by noticing that Jesus is there.

    a. How is fear creeping in to your present experience? What are his lies?
    b. In what ways have you opened yourself to guidance (false light) from the enemy? What unhealthy decisions have you made because of it?
    c. Maybe Jesus has not come to you in a vision or dream, but He wants you to know that He is there with you in the dark. What Word of *life* has He spoken to you that can guide you through the dark?

4. Forsaken's misguided belief that Life-Giver had forsaken her and the increased influence of her enemy were producing a spiraling down (progression into greater darkness) of her emotions. I want to caution you. The healing process will involve revisiting some of the feelings connected to your abuse; however, to avoid becoming stuck there or spiraling down, remember that the Holy Spirit is with you in the darkness. That is truth and any message that opposes that is a lie. If we retreat into the lie an internal and external isolation can take place that will lead to greater hopelessness. The Holy Spirit is waiting to comfort you and bring you hope.

    a. In Forsaken's vulnerable state the emotions that accompanied her abuses were beginning to surface: the empty feel-

ing in her gut, fear, loneliness and doubt. What emotions are you presently feeling that are connected to your abuse?
   b. What is the truth concerning these emotions? What is the lie?
   c. In what ways can you receive comfort and strength from the Holy Spirit?

5. In the dream, Life-Giver is depicted as both strong and compassionate. He is shown as the One who leads an army to fight for her, but also the One who weeps with her. His intention toward her and His earthly kingdom is to bring life to them, release His plans for them and counter the effects of Enemy King's army. *Life* and healing is found in the river that flows out from Life-Giver's throne. We have to choose to get in, however, by riding along with Life-Giver on Hope and seeing through His eyes.

   a. In what ways do you see Jesus as being both strong and compassionate in your life and circumstances?
   b. Are you allowing Jesus to take you into His river? What refreshing or healing are you receiving?
   c. What difference does it make in your experience to know that there is a heavenly army that fights for you?

Chapter Four

A DARKENED ABODE

I pray to you, O Lord, my rock. Do not turn a deaf ear to me. For if you are silent, I might as well give up and die. Listen to my prayer for mercy as I cry out to you for help, as I lift my hands toward your holy sanctuary (Psalm 28:1–2, NLT).

The bleak night once more encroached upon the valley as Forsaken and Despair uncertainly maneuvered their way down the partially concealed trail. Forsaken noted to herself that in spite of the lantern Despair held in front of her, the footpath had taken on a more malicious character. Jagged rocks jutted through the soles of her shoes and sliced the bottom of her feet; thorns of concealed branches pierced her flesh. And the hand of this companion, Despair, grew colder as Forsaken committed her way to him.

Jolted by the additional and sustained pain, Forsaken succumbed to a fleeting thought. She considered, "I wonder if I can find a way to flee into the darkness and conceal my broken body from my enemy."

Despair, recognizing her intention, grinned as he tightened his grip on her.

Forsaken promptly concluded, "I have wandered such a long way from Life-Giver. I am certain He won't pursue me here."

Yet, the Spirit of Life-Giver was never far behind. He was grieved by her contemplations; nevertheless, He was dedicated to remain secretly by her side and watch for opportunities to help. Life-Giver's plan was true to His character—to reveal to her His endless love even though she had strayed far from it.

Despair had a different intention. As was true of his nasty character, he kept repeating a somber monologue describing Forsaken's unhappy past as they traveled on together. "Pity on you, Ms Forsaken, that your Life-Giver would lead you to such a place as this. Indeed, yours is a woeful state."

Oh yes, he persuasively and deceptively presented his words to showcase his *sorrow* over her pitiful condition, but his true intent, largely hidden from Forsaken, would one day be uncovered as adversarial.

At Despair's bidding, Pain, Doubt, Abuse and Death, who had sworn their allegiance to him, came and huddled around Forsaken. Her response, provoked by their presence, was expected. She plunged into a strange heaviness that swept over her like a dense fog. This heaviness evoked all the contemptible emotions that were housed within her and that she had worked so hard to suppress: anger, self-hatred, shame, sadness, regret, fury, loneliness, anguish and fear. Like a torrent from hell, they rushed through her deepening her despair. Though fully clothed, she suddenly felt naked and exposed in the night air.

Minutes mimicked hours in which Forsaken stood frozen in the wake of this attack. Unable to hide or run, she fled into the internal safety of her mind where momentary relief was sought. "There the darkness will hide me," she argued, "and no one will see or hurt me."

Forsaken secretly tunneled her way deep inside and when she reached an obscure place, she remained. There she sat, huddled in a corner secured by a blanket of peace offered to her by her own mind. Momentary relief was halted, however, when a tug from Despair's hand shocked her back into her external existence. The fate of her life, presently determined by this darkened path, grieved Forsaken and her thoughts turned towards death once more. "I wish I could just slip into a place where pain would not define my existence. This despair is just too great!"

That was an invitation for Death to hasten a move, but as he did so, the Spirit quickly lunged between him and Forsaken. Death's anger was fierce. The fury in his eyes exposed the madness he was about to unleash on Forsaken. Right then the Spirit's righteous anger rose up against

Death. The blast of the Spirit's breath alone was sufficient force to thrust Death backwards, causing him to fall. Observing the conflict, Despair cleverly stepped away from Forsaken.

Forsaken was largely unaware of what had just transpired in the unseen world, although her body registered the reprieve. Responding to the new sense of ease, she decided, "I think I can travel on now. I don't know why, but I don't feel quite as tormented as before."

As Despair led the entourage down the path, the Spirit claimed a place at Forsaken's side and released a life-giving force to her as He gently embraced her. Conceding to a temporary setback, Despair moved a few more paces ahead. He did so tentatively, not wanting to invite open conflict with the Spirit that would damage his rapport with Forsaken. He remained continually alert, though, as he protested to himself, "I have to find a way to entice Forsaken away from the Spirit. The aid He is giving her is dangerous to my plan. I already see too much life coming into her body."

With the help of the Spirit, Forsaken established a new diligence to the course. She was able to clear her head a bit and thoughts of *life* on the other side of the valley returned. "That's right, Life-Giver did promise me *life* and not death," she remembered.

Despair realized his urgent need to devise a plan. Death, still infuriated by his confrontation with the Spirit, imagined a scheme. He plotted with Despair, "Let's take her by way of the ravine. I don't need to remind you that it is the most hazardous path in this valley and furthermore," he growled, "I can make certain she will never evade its captivity."

Despair boasted, "That plan is flawless. She will be doomed for certain! Let's go." Both Death and Despair joined arms and efforts to lead Forsaken to her intended destruction.

Forsaken soon recognized that the footpath was narrowing and declining severely. The scene was far from majestic. Rock, brush and fallen debris formed a wall to her right and seemed to loom over her, threatening her forward momentum. To her left the footpath dropped off into a deep ravine. She was not sure of its depth because of the degree of darkness that engulfed her. Even with the lantern that Despair carried, she could barely view the next place to plant her feet.

At one spot, Despair speculated, "I'll position this lantern in front of my body. Then Forsaken will have no light to guide her steps!" His stunt was successful. Forsaken lost her footing which nearly propelled her down into the deadly ravine. She was saved when the Spirit, unknown to her, guided her hand to a sturdy branch that was protruding from the mountain wall.

Forsaken moved on in silence as her movements became more and more restricted. Severely shaken from her near fall, she clung, helplessly, to the damp jagged wall while she gripped the protruding twigs and rocks as gods. In many places she inched her back nervously along the wall, seeking greater stability. Despair had gained a great advantage on her and had moved far ahead, but that did not trouble her. The only thing she hoped for now was the sweet solace of isolation.

"All of you get out of here and leave me alone," she wanted to scream, but she didn't dare. Her head was pounding. She was tired of this journey, tired of the empty promises, tired of the mental torment, and she was very tired of her traveling companions.

"Where are You Life-Giver?" She replayed those familiar words in her mind again and again.

Pain leaned in and whispered, "That's right, Forsaken, the pain in your body and soul is proof. He's not here."

Tears flooded Forsaken's eyes and she became increasingly blinded. This caused her to be unaware of her surroundings, her fears, and most importantly the truth. The only thing that kept her attention this moment was her pain: physical, emotional and spiritual. She was drowning in it. She couldn't envision anything else.

"Why did you do this to me?" she cried out. There were *many* more cries inside, but that one cry was all she had energy to expel.

Then, as she stood fixed against the wall, the cries inside began to break loose. One by one they began to shake her internal structure and demand recognition. Forsaken couldn't control the quaking in her body, which began in her feet and rapidly forged its way up her body. In fear, she asked herself, "Where is this going? It is too big for me to contain anymore. This darkness will have to help me contain it."

At that thought, she began to grab at the wall for rocks and began hurling them into the darkness covering the ravine. And from the surging pit within, she began to shout, "I hate you for hurting me! I hate you for shaming me! I hate you for leaving me…" Her screams went on and on and on.

Forsaken anxiously shuffled along the wall, seizing more rocks and flinging them out into the night along with her bold proclamations. Her tears escaped unrestrained. Anger mixed with sadness, violence mixed with helplessness and bitterness mixed with fear. Those were giant emotions for such a little girl; although now, it seemed the immense silence became attentive to her cries.

"Will that be enough to satisfy me?" she asked herself. "At least for now it must," came the reply from within. In actuality, she wasn't sure what would satisfy her aching heart.

She remained rigidly adhered to the wall until the tears and the quaking stopped, until her skin stopped exploding and the pain eased. The emptiness was the only thing that remained—this deep startling void in the core of her being. She longed to find something or someone else inhabiting that space. She longed for an answer to her deepest cries from the great unknown. Nevertheless, there came no reply.

"Why is there no answer to my plea?" she thought. "Am I not worthy enough?" Forsaken rapidly dismissed those thoughts, however. She was beyond asking. "The deep agony that comes with asking and not receiving is too much for me to bear," she reasoned. As she allowed her body to slowly slip down the wall, she quietly slipped away into the deep inner despair that she had uncovered. Alone, she sat motionless staring into the enormous expanse of nothingness that mirrored her soul.

Time held no relevance in that place. She knew that eventually her body would get up and travel on, although right now she could not reason how. The strong emotions she had experienced only moments ago were replaced by a quiet, albeit seductive, resignation that seeped into every part of her being and settled in her heart. She thought it odd to remember that after the abuse she had experienced this very same feeling.

"It is like being captured in a void," she thought, "a molecule of time where nothing appears as it actually is and the future is irrelevant." There she remained—in her thoughts, but outside of her thoughts—mesmerized in a dreary bliss.

Forsaken was barely aware that Despair came back for her, helped her up and urged her to move along. Movement seemed difficult, but she was not alarmed by this. Her arms and legs yielded solely to the commands of the mind. All other assessments concerning her present state were removed from her consciousness.

Throughout the next number of days Forsaken's drone-like existence remained unchanged. Despair kept pushing her on and cunningly guided her to a path that descended into the ravine. Forsaken was blinded to his plan and willingly followed him. Despair stopped only occasionally to drink or eat (from Forsaken's bread and juice) or to sleep just a little bit at night.

Rest was not in Despair's plan. He determined to take advantage of Forsaken's broken condition and further wear her down. He was delighted to notice that Forsaken rejected any attempts to gain assistance from the Spirit—either directly or indirectly. Even so, that did not deter the Spirit from remaining in close proximity, waiting for the time when Forsaken would ask for Him.

"I promised Life-Giver I would travel near to her and I am faithful to My promise," the Spirit stated aloud in earshot of Despair and his entourage.

Sadly, Forsaken could not hear Him and her heart grew more and more reclusive as the days progressed. A strange mournfulness accompanied her now, which gained strength as they penetrated deeper into the ravine. Forsaken could no longer distinguish day from night through the gray foggy mist that had settled into the area. Sometimes she just wandered around a bit until Despair grabbed her and brought her back on course. Her other companions (Pain, Doubt, Abuse and Death) traveled at a distance. They now recognized that there was no need for their immediate interventions. They had succeeded in bringing Forsaken to a place of utter retreat from the Spirit where her own dejected mind was set against her.

Her thoughts ran rampant at this juncture in the journey. She neither desired nor possessed the energy to harness their endless harassment of her: "You are no good. You are not worth Life-Giver's attention. You have no power to change. Look at the darkness around you. That is all there is. Why bother trying anymore."

The shame and self-contempt which had remained as a residue from the abuse, as well as the shame accompanying her present condition, were systematically stripping her of her self-identity and any trace of dignity her soul may have struggled to retain. She desired only the peace that non-existence would bring and, at the recognition of that thought, she began a desperate search for some sort of darkened hide-a-way in this corrupt valley.

Forsaken and Despair had traveled silently for some time now. Despair purposely was not engaging in conversation to give Forsaken the opportunity to rehearse her self-denigrating thoughts. Forsaken had slowed her steps due to her weakened condition, and Despair matched her pace while still keeping ahead of her. Despair remained in control of the lantern, which was fine with Forsaken, even on those occasions when he traveled a distance ahead. Forsaken embraced and befriended the darkness because it seemed to conceal her shame.

As Despair led the way around a sharp curve, Forsaken thought she noticed an opening in the rock wall. "Could this be my route of escape?" she questioned herself as she further slowed her pace in an attempt to lose Despair.

Her strategy succeeded. Despair walked by the opening and had proceeded a good distance down the path before Forsaken arrived at that place. Lowering her head to look into the opening, she inwardly confirmed, "I was right. This is a hidden cavern." Not realizing what she was doing, but drawn in by her own helplessness and shame, she inched her body through the opening and quickly crept into the mouth of the cave.

Mesmerized by her hasty decision and half crazed from her lengthy journey, she thought only of protecting herself from Despair and her other dark companions. She began to feel her way around the floor of this internal sanctuary, frantically seeking something she could use to dam up the opening. She was repulsed by a slimy substance on the cavern floor and had to force herself to run her fingers through the muck searching for a hidden treasure that could save her. She could find none. In desperation she started racing her hands over the interior walls. Protruding rocks pierced her feeble hands as she aggressively inspected the wall.

"What am I doing?" she thought. "Safety, safety, safety," her mind replayed her only sought-after goal. The gnawing fear that she would be unable to achieve safety grew larger and larger.

Her body trembling, she increased the intensity of the search. Too quickly, her fierce determination faded into futility. The walls of the cavern seemed to extend their presence over and around her, as if to imprint her unwarranted fate upon her. Engulfed in their presence and scarcely able to breathe, she sat stunned for a moment on the murky floor.

Unknown to her, Shame and Fear, her *new* companions, approached and sat on either side of Forsaken. Fear was no stranger to her, however. His lies had woven their way into her heart from the time of Abuse's attack until now. Joining forces with his evil companion Doubt, Fear had convinced Forsaken that *Life-Giver's* intentions were evil. Now he sat in silence, gleefully recognizing the enormity of the fear already present in Forsaken's heart.

Shame, on the other hand, spoke immediately, "You made a good choice to enter this cave. Finally, you are alone with your unmet sorrow. Now, the agony of your sin and self-hatred can be unleashed into your secret abode—a fit attendant for your blackened heart."

Forsaken could have argued, but she knew the voice to be true. She agonized, "I have blackened my heart. My sin and shame have overtaken me. And this is where it has led me—to this darkened cave." She remained there, caught in contemplation, until the sound of voices startled her and brought her back into her present reality.

"Oh, no, Despair is coming for me," she murmured aloud. Suddenly, an idea grasped her mind. "The rocks… I can use the rocks to block the entrance…if only they are loose enough." She groped at one rock and then another, but they would not loosen.

Fear and Shame turned to each other. Shame inquired of Fear, "What shall we do? I can convince her that she is worthless if we can keep her hidden with us in this cave."

Fear concurred. He realized he would have more influence over her mind if she remained trapped in their presence. Therefore he persuaded her, "Forsaken, keep trying. Here's a rock—try this one."

Forsaken, focused only on the desire to gain whatever covering and safety she could manage, grabbed the loosened rock and frenetically secured the opening of the cave. Fatigued from the expended energy, her body slumped back against the rock wall and unknowingly into the welcoming arms of her fellow inhabitants, Fear and Shame.

Pathway **TO YOUR HEALING**

1. A common emotion following abuse is false shame. What is the difference between false shame and true shame? True shame alerts us to a wrong that we have committed. When we confess it to God and change our behavior, the feelings of shame are eliminated. False shame, on the other hand, can come from a wrong done to us. Repentance will not lead to a lifting of the shameful feelings because the cause is the trauma. Abuse produces feelings of worthlessness and self-contempt ("there is something really wrong with me") and fuels false shame. The remedy is to receive God's grace and to accept ourselves. If we fail to do that, we may act out in unhealthy hiding.

    a. Forsaken moved in and out of the place of believing the enemy's lies. As she embraced self-contempt, she lost her sense of a healthy identity and saw herself as the enemy saw her—worthless! Are you walking in who you are in Christ, or have you embraced self-contempt?

    b. Forsaken was motivated by her false shame to find a hiding place. At first, isolation can feel like a worthy covering, but in the end it leads to loneliness and more false shame. Are you seeking to cover yourself in unhealthy ways? Can you describe what those unhealthy ways look like?

    c. False shame produces feelings of vulnerability and a sense of exposure. Forsaken was desperate to create a place of safety for herself. She did not care that it was a darkened cave. Are you feeling vulnerable or unsafe? What healthy ways can you choose to gain safety, instead of picking a cave?

2. Abuse produces all kinds of negative emotions that need to be processed for the recovering person to move into health.

Forsaken had attempted to repress those emotions for some time, though her defenses started breaking down and she had to face what was housed within.

Processing our emotions involves several steps: acknowledging the emotion, speaking with someone else about it, allowing the Lord in to heal it, and releasing lies or attachments that are connected to the trauma. For Forsaken to move toward healing, she first had to acknowledge and express her internal agony. Since she was running from her pain, she was forced to experience the feelings when her defenses started breaking down. A better way is to embrace the pain and find someone to walk through it with you. I remind you, the Holy Spirit is always close and ready to help you.

    a. Are you running from your pain like Forsaken did, or are you ready to embrace it and talk about it? Do you have someone to do that with?

    b. Journaling is another way to express your internal agony. This week, journal about your abuse and share it with one other person.

    c. Like Forsaken, you may have experienced one abuse on top of another or prolonged abuse. If that is you, your internal negative emotions may feel too big or too scary to express. Please get professional help from a therapist, minister or support group to guide you through. There is nothing weak or ungodly about needing help. Just make sure that the person is familiar with abuse recovery.

3. The longer we turn from God and follow the ways of the enemy, the darker the path will become. Forsaken moved further and further away from Life-Giver and became deaf to the voice of the Spirit. In that process she traveled through despair, but finally arrived at a state of resignation. She didn't care what happened to her and she wandered aimlessly about. This can be associated with: (1) a severing of one's emotions (repression), (2) the emotions or the entire event becoming packaged in the

psyche (dissociation: the example in text of Forsaken climbing into her mind for solace), or (3) the person disconnecting from their body (depersonalization). These are all defenses against the pain. At the time of the event they were functional mechanisms, although later these defenses hinder the person's ability to connect to themselves or others in their lives from their true self.

    a. Have you experienced resignation in the past, or are you presently experiencing a state of resignation? What is this like for you?
    b. Have you experienced repression, dissociation or depersonalization in the past or present? What is (was) this experience like for you?
    c. If that is not your experience, have you recognized times when you practiced ignoring, denying or numbing your emotions? What is (was) this experience like for you?

4. The goal in this process is to acknowledge and receive healing for the damaged emotions whereby maintaining our connection with our true self. Forsaken decided to hide in a cave. We can be like her and withdraw physically from others into isolation or we can withdraw inside of ourselves and develop false selves through which we meet the world. Both stances are equally damaging because the true self with its pain and fear gets buried more and more deeply within. The Spirit longs to connect with our true self and bring healing, but this too becomes difficult because of the barriers.

    a. Are there places that you hide your true self? What kind of cave have you chosen? What is your false self like?
    b. Are you ready to invite the Holy Spirit into those places? He is waiting for you to ask Him.
    c. Sometimes coming out of hiding is a gradual process. What small step can you take today?

5. Forsaken had traveled so far from Life-Giver that she couldn't believe that He would pursue her in that wayward place. She lost hope. From that hopeless state she embraced the darkness even more. Her thoughts were consumed with her disappointment and her desire for non-existence. As she retreated inside of herself, the only thing she found was the deep internal void created by her abuse and neglect. The Spirit wanted to inhabit that void, but Forsaken did not realize that fact.

   a. The emotional damage resulting from abuse can be widespread. One occurrence that is common is the sense of an internal void or emptiness. This can be caused from neglect, abandonment or lack of protection (especially by parents). It can also be the result of a disconnection from oneself and others due to the shame and self-contempt. The experience of loss can also contribute to the void (loss of innocence, health, worth, goals or dreams). Are you (present or past) experiencing that void? What do you think are the contributing factors for you?
   b. Forsaken was incorrect in her assessment that Life-Giver could not pursue her or travel into the dark places. Jesus, by His Spirit, will always pursue us and there is no darkness that will keep Him out. Sometimes our emotions lie, however. Do you think your emotions are lying to you? In what ways?
   c. As Death whispered his lies to Forsaken, she had to remind herself of the promise of *life* spoken to her by Life-Giver. What promise can you remind yourself of today?

Chapter Five

A TURNED HEART

> *"Cast away from you all the transgressions which you have committed, and get yourselves a new heart and a new spirit. For why should you die, O house of Israel? For I have no pleasure in the death of one who dies,"* says the Lord God. *"Therefore turn and live!"* (Ezekiel 18:31–32).

Forsaken, still unsettled from her escape into her hidden domain, sat unmoved against the inner cavern wall. Her nervous frenzy, now stubbornly contained in her stilled body, was nonetheless readied for an attack from Despair should he tunnel through the debris to retrieve her. Reprieve from her nightmarish existence was not yet evident and her heart raced excessively attesting to that fact. In spite of the darkness, she fixed her eyes on the makeshift blockade and struggled to gain some sense of control over body and mind.

"How did I get here?" she complained loudly, chastising herself. "This is not where I intentionally wanted to be. When did my heart deceive me? How will I ever get back? It is so far!"

"That's right," Fear flatly interrupted. "It is too far back. Your heart has led you to this *forsaken* place and there's no way back. Don't even think you can…"

His fatalistic words were interrupted by the deafening sound of rock striking rock. With each strike the walls of the cavern reverberated and sent the sound echoing throughout the interior and into the interior of Forsaken's heart. Involuntarily, her body stiffened. Then, as abruptly as the blasts began, they ceased. The dense silence saturated the air around her as she awaited the suspected potential danger. Forsaken's senses remained heightened, although relieved, when the next sound that she heard was garbled voices on the other side of the wall.

"Maybe I can hear if I move closer," Forsaken hoped aloud.

She dared to shift her body slightly closer to the cavern wall to determine who was speaking or distinguish what they were saying, but her attempt failed. The voices gradually became more distant until silence, once again, permeated her dwelling place. A considerable time elapsed after the last sounds were heard before Forsaken would admit to herself that she was safe—at least for the moment. As she haltingly relaxed her back against the rock wall, she exhaled a deep breath of air into her shallow habitat.

For the first time, Forsaken attuned herself to her immediate surroundings and recognized that her new dwelling place was severely restrictive. From where she was sitting against a wall, she could stretch out her legs and touch the other wall. She determined not to explore any further, though, until she rested awhile. She hoped Despair and the others would not be back any time soon. (She wasn't totally sure who the "others" were, but she guessed they were Death, Abuse, Pain and Doubt.) In spite of her cramped condition and her lingering fears, Forsaken fell quickly into a thoroughly engaging and uncontested sleep. She did not remain there long, however, and awoke only to find herself looking straight into the face of Fear.

Fear had remained alert during Forsaken's sleep and had continued jabbing her mind and body with his taunts until she was alerted to his intrusion. Now lifeless, her limbs weighted under the presence of Fear, she lay anchored to the cavern floor—defenseless against her present adversary.

"How can I withstand this encounter with such a fiendish force?" she thought. An overall sense of powerlessness swept through her whole being as Fear continued his pervasive attack.

"Look at yourself now, Forsaken," he badgered. "You thought you were afraid before! Look at where you are now. There is no escape from me. You cannot hide from me."

As Fear taunted her persistently with his hideous lies, Forsaken noticed something that alarmed her. Although she hated his lies, it was his actual presence that paralyzed her and kept her from any movement that would aid her cause. "This presence reminds me of the terror I felt during the attack from Abuse. I fear that my body will never escape this horror," she admitted with reservation.

As her thought processes yielded to the influence of Fear and Shame, she began to lose touch with her whereabouts. The guarantee of security she had hoped for inside the cave's protective walls now evaded her as she fixed her eyes on its impenetrable walls. "I not only have lost my freedom," she groaned, "I have yet to discover what this darkness holds for me. Can I stop this darkness from invading my body and soul?"

Fear, with signs of victory flashing through his eyes, consulted with Shame, "Now is the time to execute Enemy King's plan. We can hold Forsaken captive to the darkness and to Enemy King forever!" They both agreed and proceeded to arm themselves with their greatest weaponry.

Shame attacked her first. Immediately, the weight of her scarred existence consumed her. Forsaken was sure, if she had enough light to view her skin that she would see the marks left there by Abuse: unworthy, hatred of self, hopeless, unclean, unwanted, ugly, suspicious, insane and empty. She had been convinced years before that those scars to her heart and soul were visible to the outside world; because of those convictions, she had increasingly hid herself until the logical thing to do was to leave Life-Giver's home and kingdom. As she sat in the presence of Shame, she declared with greater reserve, "Those scars are all I will ever be."

With that proclamation, Shame secretly seized a place close to Forsaken's side and endorsed her assessment by stating, "That's right, Forsaken, those scars will always determine your worth."

Fear stabbed at her heart and repeated his taunts. "You will never escape the fear I planted in your heart."

Hearing that, Forsaken yielded even more to her deepening depression, banishing the small bits of herself that still embraced life into the dark interior of her soul.

"I don't dare hope for life," breathed Forsaken.

The atmosphere in the cave now thickened under the weight of Forsaken's distress. She sat there dazed by the contemplations of her mind as it issued its complaints. Drawing her knees to her chest, she felt small, frail and helpless. "Where is Life-Giver now? I guess He could never follow me here…to this awful place," she agonized.

The Spirit (who had never left her, even when she entered the cave) was moved by her plea and whispered, "I'm here. I've never left you."

But Forsaken could not hear. Her bitterness had erected a wall around her heart that blocked the voice of the Spirit. The Spirit persisted in His pursuit. He moved close to her, bent low and breathed a puff of hope into her faint heart. As He did so, her heart gained enough spiritual attunement to hear His voice once again.

"You are Cherished," He whispered.

Forsaken was shocked, elated and bewildered by the Spirit's voice: "How was He able to enter with me into this hidden place? And why is He calling me "Cherished" while I am in this shameful state?"

The Spirit lovingly responded, "It will take us time to turn your heart, but it is very attainable! I want to help you."

Forsaken desired greatly to believe Him, even though her heart struggled against it. But as she sat with the Spirit and examined her heart, she decided she wanted to try His way. She inhaled a large, deep breath and made a bold declaration, "I am so horrified that I listened to my estranged heart, and this is where it has led me. I don't know if there's another way, but I am ready for another way."

With that utterance the Spirit became alerted that Forsaken was ready for His intervention. When He asked her, "Is it OK if we begin the work now?" she answered "Yes!" with an eagerness that surprised her. Forsaken understood that Enemy King's army had contributed greatly to her despised disposition; nevertheless, urged by the Spirit, she strove to understand her own troublesome actions and their contribution to her demise.

Focusing on the rock walls which surrounded Forsaken, the Spirit began to gently remind her of the walls she had intentionally and unintentionally constructed in her heart. She had erected them one by one from the rocks that others had hurled at her (insults, blame, shame, rejection, abandonment) and from rocks she hurled at others or herself (anger, hatred, mistrust, self-protection, self-destruction). With the Spirit's help she sat and reflected on those awhile, not in the self-condemning way she had previously, but in a kinder way that *began* a gradual process of softening her heart.

She breathed a prayer of repentance, "I'm sorry, Life-Giver, for the resentment I have held toward others in response to my hurt. I'm sorry for the ways I have shamed and harmed myself. But, most of all, I am sorry for the accusations I have hurled at You." Forsaken wished that she could tell those things to Life-Giver personally; although, even speaking those words aloud brought a great sense of relief to her soul. Furthermore, when she looked inside at the barrier around her heart she noticed a portion of it had been destroyed.

Forsaken meditated on that discovery until a strange phenomenon brought her attention back to her surroundings. Her darkened shelter appeared somewhat brighter! The walls of the cavern were now faintly visible as she carefully surveyed its perimeter. Unable to determine the cause of this occurrence, but grateful for it, Forsaken began to explore the dimly lit cave that she could just barely see now.

"Darn that Spirit," Shame clamored to Fear. "How did *He* get in here? I can't stand *His* light!"

Fear and Shame darted towards the mouth of the cave where they hid themselves in a shadowy corner behind some fallen debris. "The last thing I want is to be noticed by the Spirit," griped Fear, remembering that his past encounter with the Spirit was anything but good.

Despite the stiffness in her body from sitting too long, Forsaken felt drawn by the Spirit to kneel. With difficulty, she adjusted her body until she could get in that position. As she remained there on her knees, the Spirit spoke with her again. In a tone so respectful and kind, He said, "Forsaken, I need to show you some things that may hurt you, although this truth has the power to heal you."

Her heart was willing to listen, so she leaned in closer to the Spirit to hear more clearly. He continued, "I want you to see each untruth your heart embraced and each encounter where you failed to live guided and empowered by Me."

As Forsaken agreed, each failure was revealed to her, one by one. However, it was not like the harsh accusations Enemy King and his servants often brought to her. This exposure to the truth was full of gentleness and grace—so characteristic of Life-Giver and His Spirit.

Forsaken slowly and painfully maneuvered her mind through each untruth she had believed, and she haltingly guided her heart through each failure. Gradually, a righteous sorrow began trickling its way into her consciousness and she began to weep softly as she yielded to the Spirit's revelations. As she persisted in this soul-searching posture, a delightful quietness began to settle into her heart and mind replacing the debilitating conflict, confusion and despair. Peace coming from the Spirit's heart engaged her heart and He invited her to receive the comfort she had been striving for. "Forsaken, I have been longing to impart My comfort to you, but you were not ready. There were times when you blocked the consolation I longed to give you."

Forsaken looked away and lowered her head. The Spirit encouraged her, "Don't be saddened, dear one. Now, I am happy. I can see your surrendered heart and I am glad! Open your heart in trust to Life-Giver and I will fill it."

Delighted, Forsaken lifted her head and declared, "Yes, I will trust again. I will trust Life-Giver!"

The Spirit, who was moved by her confession, drew very near to her and lovingly deposited Life-Giver's deep, compassionate and uncompromising love into her newly-opened heart. Gradually, like someone arousing from a deep sleep, Forsaken's heart awakened to this unhindered and unwavering love. She remained breathless, stunned by this endearing Presence who was rescuing her heart from the dreaded coldness that had held her heart captive for so long. Saddened by her resistance to His presence in the past, yet exceedingly grateful for love's pursuit, she quietly, gently, but assuredly embraced what the Spirit was imparting to her.

"I don't understand this kind of love," she thought, "but I am forever grateful that His love searched for me, even in my dreadful condition. How can I not respond to Him? My yielded heart has never felt so full."

Forsaken found the Spirit's drawing of her heart inescapable though desirable as He elicited more and more of her heart. She gave it willingly, however, as her deep passion for Life-Giver became ignited and increased.

"How can I find a way back to Life-Giver?" she questioned aloud. "I must find a way to somehow give this great love back to Him."

Her thoughts turned, once more, to the luxurious land on the other side of the valley and the new life that Life-Giver had promised her. She dared to entertain those thoughts, now, as the Spirit spoke His confirmation to her heart, "Yes, Forsaken, that new life *is* still possible. Believe the promise!" Knowing that Forsaken was now ready to ingest truth, the Spirit urged her, "Remember Life-Giver's Promise Book, Forsaken, and how much you love His promises. They are right there in your bag."

Forsaken's heart was stirred as she recalled the promises she liked the most and the ones that earlier had brought her such strength. "I am so glad for that memory," she confessed. "Maybe His promises will help me now."

She laboriously shifted her weight from her knees and began the meticulous search for her belongings. "I hope there is enough light in this cavern for me to read. I must try."

Forsaken did not remember pulling her bag into the cave with her; although, she couldn't imagine herself leaving it behind. She became disheartened, however, when a thorough search proved fruitless. She was ready to stop looking when the Spirit prompted her to scan the cavern one more time. Unwilling to be disappointed, but willing to be obedient to the Spirit, she continued her pursuit. Then she saw it! Excitement seized her heart. There was her bag, stuffed behind some fallen rocks and debris in a darkened corner where Fear and Shame had hidden it.

Forsaken feverishly rummaged through the contents hoping that Life-Giver's Promise Book would still be there. Pleased and amazed at her own pleasure, she grasped the book at the bottom of the bag and pulled it out. Before opening the book she inquired aloud, "Life-Giver, what promise do You want me to see today?" With an eagerness she admittedly had not experienced for a considerable time, she opened the Promise Book.

There were certain pages that seemed to bulge a little. Her curiosity piqued, she carefully opened the book to that place. Forsaken found that Life-Giver had pressed a beautiful white rose between the pages and included a hand-written note on exquisite stationery. Confused as to whether she should read it or not (she did not want to invade Life-Giver's privacy), she stared aimlessly at the page until one word captured her interest. At the very top of the note was inscribed the name *Cherished*. She couldn't believe her eyes—Cherished!

"Life-Giver wrote a note to me?" she thought, half in disbelief and half in excitement. Giving it her full attention, she picked up the note and began to read:

Cherished

My Cherished one, My love for you
Is tender as the rose.
Behold, how sweet the blossom is
How lavishly it grows.

Why do you turn away from Me
And hide yourself in shame?
When I would come and lift you
up—I do not come to blame.

I know the hurt and all the
pain—I traveled that way, too,
So that now I could be with you
And help to bring you through.

You may not recognize, at first,
My purposes and plans.
But, do not worry My dear child—
You are safe in My hands.

All that I ask of you, My child,
Is that you come and rest.
Can you trust Me, now, to love you?
Come, lie upon My breast.

Love, Life-Giver

Forsaken sat in silence while exploring her heart. "Can I really trust and rest in Life-Giver like the poem says? I can feel His loving embrace, but can I trust it?"

Then as she glanced down at the paper, she realized there was a P.S. on the bottom that stated, "Read the promise on this page." Her eyes scanned the page until she came to one promise that was circled.

She read it aloud: "The Lord redeems the soul of His servants, and none of those who trust in Him shall be condemned" (Psalm 34:22).

"That includes *me*," she said as she courageously invited hope and trust to move into her recovering heart.

Pathway **TO YOUR HEALING**

1. Forsaken had arrived at her final state of confinement, but she had several severe limitations. Her emotions had been badly damaged from her past abuse and she had not received the proper healing. This had caused her to digress to this ultimate place of fear and entrapment. (If we allow our damaged emotions to go untouched, they will eventually entrap us.) In that sickened state her heart had made unwise choices concerning her relationship with Life-Giver and her relationship with her internal pain. While her goal had been to protect herself by hiding from her pain and shame, her act of hiding actually resulted in greater captivity by her enemy. The enemy enters into and cooperates with our sickened state and our poor choices.

   a. What emotions still need your attention and healing from the Lord? Can you describe their progression into their sickened state?
   b. What is the state of your heart? Are there unwise choices you have made concerning your relationship with Jesus and your relationship with your pain? What are they?
   c. How has the enemy influenced your poor choices?

2. Forsaken had not predicted as she struggled to hide herself from her enemies of Despair, Death, Abuse, Pain and Doubt, that she could not hide from her other enemies of Fear and Shame. In fact, it was Fear and Shame who had enticed her into hiding. Forsaken had moved hastily and had not waited for the Spirit

to direct her. As she was led into her captive state she recognized that her heart had deceived her. Her own resources were inferior to challenging the enemy. The more she attempted to *defend herself*, the greater her captivity became.

   a. Your defenses may be walls of isolation or denial or other forms of escaping your pain. What ways have you attempted to *defend yourself*? How has the enemy used that against you?
   b. Forsaken had thought she was successful in locking her enemy away. She could faintly hear their voices on the other side of the wall. Then their voices became garbled and faded away. The enemy wanted her to believe she was safe. But the voice of the enemy became clear again, through Fear and Shame, and her entrapment became even greater. What is your experience with the deception of the enemy? Has he cleverly deceived you into believing you no longer have to fight him? (That is Satan's deception to the body of Christ. He wants us to believe he is not there so that we will not be alert to his influence.)
   c. Forsaken's own resources were ineffective against her enemy. She needed Life-Giver's Spirit to direct her and empower her against her enemy. What are the resources you have used that have been ineffective? Can you ask the Holy Spirit to give you His tools to fight your enemy?

3. Forsaken finally declared that she desired a different way. She not only came to an end of her resources, but she also recognized that she wanted to set her heart in another direction. The Spirit saw that she was ready to receive from Him, and so He could act in her to a greater degree. (He had never left her side, though His power was limited due to her hardened heart.) He gave Forsaken hope by reviving her heart and revealing to her the steps out of her entrapment. Since she was ready to hear, they could act together to bring her the healing and freedom that she desired.

    a. Have you hardened your heart to the ways of the Lord? In what ways?
    b. Are you ready for your heart to turn around?
    c. What help from the Spirit do you need for this to happen? Can you ask Him for it?

4. Healing of the heart is a gradual process, but the Holy Spirit is very able to perform it. Prior to her heart change, Forsaken believed the enemy's assessment that the scars of her abuse would remain and determine her worth forever. Nevertheless, with the Spirit's help she was able to believe and embrace the truth that Life-Giver had a greater destiny for her. She was also able to embrace the correction of the Spirit. He desired to gently reveal to her the decisions she had made that agreed with her enemies and had entrapped her in her pain. Forsaken found that when the Spirit corrects us, He does it without the condemnation or shame that the enemy brings.

    a. What scars from your abuse did you believe were visible to others and that you would have to live with forever?
    b. Can you invite the Holy Spirit to correct your false beliefs and agreements with the lies? What is He showing you?
    c. What attitudes of heart do you need to repent of? Can you do that?

5. As Forsaken continued to search her soul, the Spirit revealed to her the rocks she had collected to help build the wall around her heart. There were the insults, blame, shame, rejection and abandonment she had received from others that she was not able to release. Furthermore, the walls contained the resentments, hatred, mistrust and blame toward Life-Giver and others; they also contained the self-blame, self-protection and self-destruction toward herself. With her heart now submitted to Life-Giver, Forsaken was able to give Life-Giver each one of those *hardened responses*, and the Spirit began softening her heart.

a. What are the walls around your heart made of? What *hardened responses* have you been holding on to?
b. Can you trust Jesus enough to give Him those hardened places? He is ready to receive them.
c. Ask the Holy Spirit to heal those places and bring His light into the darkness. He did it for Forsaken; He will do it for you.

6. The Life-Giver (through the Spirit) extended His love to Forsaken. She was surprised to discover that His love had followed her even when her heart had become unreceptive. However, now her repentant heart had opened a way for the peace and comfort she had longed for. From that surrendered place, Forsaken made a decision to trust Life-Giver again. The Spirit was delighted and renewed the promise spoken to her by Life-Giver—the promise of *life*. Forsaken's thoughts turned toward the land on the other side of the valley and she determined to find a way back to Life-Giver. As the coldness left her heart, her passion for Life-Giver was ignited once more and she longed to be with Him. She was reminded (in the note from Life-Giver) that her true identity was "Cherished"—the name Life-Giver had given her.

   a. In what ways have you noticed that the love of Jesus has followed you wherever you have gone? What was (is) that experience like for you?
   b. Can you open to the peace and comfort of the Holy Spirit? What promise does the Holy Spirit want to renew in your heart? Can you pray for a passion for God's Word?
   c. Will you commit your way to Jesus Christ (either for the first time or renew your trust)? Who does Christ say you are? Can you embrace that?

Chapter Six

A WAY OF ESCAPE

Forget the former things; do not dwell on the past. See, I am doing a new thing! Now it springs up; do you not perceive it? I am making a way in the desert and streams in the wasteland (Isaiah 43:18–19, NIV).

Forsaken sat quietly on the cold, murky cavern floor, although she wasn't cold anymore. Still gripping the Promise Book and the poem that Life-Giver composed just for her, she meditated on His words, "My Cherished one, My love for you is tender as the rose." Her mind rehearsed His words again and again as her heart began its journey of opening to this wonderful truth. Life-Giver's words swelled inside her heart and the heat of His passion towards her moved in to claim her soul.

She marveled at how special those words were to her right then and wondered, "How could I have ever discarded them?"

The Spirit was excited to recognize that He had greater influence over Forsaken since her heart had turned towards Life-Giver. He was ready to guide her through the rest of her journey, and from a place by her side He reassured her, "I promise I will remain with you and restore your heart."

Forsaken responded with a prayer to her beloved Life-Giver: "Life-Giver, I decide to accept my name again, Cherished, the name You gave to me. I will believe that I am cherished by You."

The Spirit, moved by her desire, and desiring that she *experience* this love from Life-Giver, touched her back in a gentle way. A wave of love washed over her.

Fear and Shame attempted to sabotage the transformation by calling, "Forsaken, Forsaken," but she refused to comply. That did not stop them from continuing, however, as they sent a barrage of degenerating thoughts into her mind. Fear shot her with, "Look around you, *Cherished*," (he sneered as he said her name) "nothing has changed. Do you think that because you change your name everything has changed?" He laughed a hideous cackle; then added, "Go ahead and look around you. You are trapped. You will never find a way out. You can say you *trust Him* all you want, but your Life-Giver will never find you here."

When it was apparent that she was not moved by Fear's remarks, Shame decided to test her. His statements were more personal. He slyly probed, "After what you've done with your body, you expect the *virtuous* Life-Giver to embrace you? Ha! Look at you, how torn and scarred you are. That is not glory running down your arms—that's filth!"

Shame always saved those words for the times when he desired the gravest impact, and they never failed to satisfy his evil expectations. Previously, those words would have sent Cherished running, hiding, and even clawing at her skin. Now, however, her heart held the wisdom of the Spirit. He was faithfully speaking truth into her heart, successfully countering her enemies' outlandish lies that had been brandished against her. To the dismay of her enemies, she dismissed every lie.

True to her new character, Cherished decided to embrace, once again, Life-Giver's promises. She recalled a truth He had taught her about building altars:

> *"An altar is a place of surrender and a place of remembrance; surrender all to Me and you will gain life. And, remember that I will meet you there."*

As Cherished acknowledged that truth to herself, a prior longing was awakened in her soul. It was a longing to meet with Life-Giver at that deeper place of complete surrender. She remembered it as a blissful place, a place of deep communion and a place where she felt complete in her union with Him. She was not sure that it was attainable again, but she admitted that she was willing to trust what the Spirit was speaking to her.

He reminded her, "Cherished, an altar is a meeting place with Life-Giver. It is a place to give Him your burdens and faults."

Wearied of the many ways her burdens and faults had come between them, she was anxious to construct an altar and lay them down. Nonetheless, this was a difficult action for her to initiate. "I remember giving Life-Giver *all* before and I was painfully disappointed," she whispered to the Spirit, not wanting Fear or Shame to hear her. She remembered the attack from Abuse and the mental torment following the attack; although now, Cherished was beginning to recognize the love accessible to her from Life-Giver. She regretted how blinded she had been to this truth. But the Spirit urged her to place that on the altar as well.

Cherished began to search the cave for loose and fallen rock to use in constructing the altar. Gathering those rocks beside her, she knelt and began her thoughtful prayer. She recalled Life-Giver's words, "First, give Me the grievous experiences of your life."

In response, Cherished laid several stones before her. "This one represents the abuse, this one the abandonment, and this one the mental anguish," she stated aloud.

Fear, recognizing the threat of her actions and desiring to deter her, flooded her mind with vivid images of those events, a previous successful tactic. As her head reeled, however, she noticed one thing—her heart no longer desired to attend to those imaginings. Free from the torment, she continued building her altar, "This rock represents the darkness and the unbelief."

Her action jabbed directly into Fear's side because he had labored so long to convince Cherished that she was without help and without Life-Giver. He reached out with an arrow to harm Cherished, but the Spirit intercepted him.

Cherished continued, "I'm sorry, Life-Giver, for my unbelief."

The Spirit answered, "You are forgiven."

Cherished then recalled Life-Giver's further instructions, "Give Me all the ways you have harmed others or yourself in thought, word or deed."

After several minutes of deep introspection, troubled, Cherished mumbled to herself, "How can I have good thoughts towards those who have harmed me?" She prayed, "Spirit, can You help me with this?"

The Spirit was eager to help her. He comforted her with the knowledge that all things were in Life-Giver's hands. Nothing went unnoticed by Him; He alone is the only *just* judge. Pausing to allow that knowledge to impact her heart, Cherished placed two more rocks into the pile and said, "This one is for all the judgments I have held against others, and this one for all the judgments against me."

When Shame heard that statement, he lunged at her heart seeking to deceive her as he always had. This time Cherished did not need the Spirit to protect her. Her renewed heart reminded Shame that she was forgiven and, therefore, immune to his condemnation. She reiterated, "Life-Giver, I give You all my self-contempt. I choose to accept Your love and forgive myself."

The Spirit was elated at her resolve and He forcefully removed Shame from her side, forbidding his return. Shame had no choice but to obey the Spirit's commands now that Cherished had decidedly rejected him. The Spirit then questioned her gently, "Cherished, can you now put on the altar all the ways you have failed to follow Life-Giver's truth?"

With that request, Cherished's heart recounted the many times she had failed Life-Giver and she began her sorrowful penitence. As she placed one stone after another on the altar, she confessed, "Life-Giver, forgive me for embracing and following after Death. And Despair. Self-destruction. Anger. Hatred. Fear." She continued piling the stones on the altar, "Doubt. Shame. Rebellion. Discontent. Hopelessness. Withdrawal." Then she added, "Forgive me for believing Enemy King's lies instead of Your marvelous truth."

After speaking that final prayer of repentance and placing the last stone on the altar, Cherished bowed her head and inquired, "Life-Giver, You said that You would meet us at the altar of surrender. Will You meet *me* here, Life-Giver? I surrender myself to You. I want life. Will You help me find a way out of my darkened existence?"

Cherished slowly raised her head. It seemed like a great weight had lifted off her body. The caverns inside her heart that had been darkened by her enemies were now filled with light that came from Life-Giver's

Spirit. Peace and contentment, which emanated from the light, saturated her body and soul and brought her to a place of perfect rest that lifted her pain and anguish. She now recognized that any future motive for action would have to originate from a place of rest, and not striving.

With her burdens lifted, Cherished turned her restored energy toward finding a pathway of escape leading out of her restricted environment. As she repeated a visual examination of her cave dwelling, her eyes stumbled on a small, shiny object peeking out from the rock, dirt and debris on the cavern floor. Its brightness held her attention and at first, she merely wondered how something could be so brilliant in this dimly lit cave. As she moved closer to it, she noticed that a stream of light was bouncing from its surface emitting a beautiful array of colors. Cherished's wonder grew to amazement as her imagination was excited by this stunning image.

The Spirit leaned over and instructed her, "There is something I want you to notice here." With her excitement peaking, she stilled herself to listen. The Spirit continued, "Observe the spectrum of colors. What does it remind you of?"

"Why, it reminds me of the rainbow," Cherished answered. Then she thought, "Life-Giver always said that the rainbow was a reminder to us of His promise of life. Maybe that's what He wants me to remember right now, that I will live and not die?" Cherished recalled Life-Giver's words in the dream, "*Life* to those inhabitants of the earthly kingdom, *life* to all those who will get into the river and *life* to those who hear My voice."

With the question in her mind, "Is that promise for me?" she dared to declare aloud: "I want life with Life-Giver more than anything else. Is Life-Giver saying I can still have it?"

The Spirit was overjoyed to answer her, "That's correct, Cherished. You will *live* with Life-Giver forever in His kingdom. That privilege was never taken from you. The enemy lied when he told you that you would never see Life-Giver or His kingdom again."

Then He added, "The vibrant colors that you see also represent the vibrancy that is still alive in you."

Cherished wrestled in her heart with that last statement. She pondered, "Surely the Spirit knows how much I have separated myself from

Life-Giver. I have not lived out His plans for me nor experienced the *vitality* that comes with daily walking close by His side. I fear that the places that were severely crushed by my enemy are forever dead."

Cherished's enemies had long ago convinced her that those *cherished* places inside of her had been destroyed or died. Despairing over the loss of her virtues and her ability to follow Life-Giver, the deadness inside her soul had consumed her until she lost sight of her own significance. She felt as though the beautiful treasures (gifts and abilities) that Life-Giver had thoughtfully placed within her were extracted by the hand of her evil enemy and banished from her forever. Shame and Death had been able to convince her that in her depleted state there was nothing of value left inside of her to save.

"So, why should your Life-Giver save you?" they had probed.

In an effort to bring Cherished's thinking into the present, the Spirit spoke softly into her ear, "Cherished, what I am telling you is truth." He reached over, captured a bit of the rainbow-colored light in His swift hand and deposited it into Cherished's heart. The Spirit then repeated His statement to her, "Cherished, what I am telling you is truth." And again, He whispered, "Cherished, I tell you the truth. The vibrancy that Life-Giver placed in you is still there. It's not dead."

Little by little, the truth seeped its way into her heart, down into the forgotten places, past the lies and hardness of heart and into a place of receptivity. Revived by the experience, Cherished's heart beat with renewed faith. She could sense walls crumbling on the inside: walls of self-protection, isolation and bitterness became defenseless under the penetration of the Spirit's light.

The light now illuminated the internal chambers of her heart. Brilliant colors danced their way off the cavern walls as they simultaneously excited her *desire* within. "Desire" is the perfect word to describe it because desire is exactly what Cherished felt had died: desire for Life-Giver, desire to be all Life-Giver created her to be, and finally desire for life. She somehow *knew* this moment was a pivotal one. Even though the internal walls were not completely demolished and her darkened existence still a reality, the Spirit's light was burning its way into her heart, creating in her a passion for the life she had been feverishly rejecting.

Energized, Cherished elected to reestablish her search for an escape route leading out of the cave. Because of the light she had a newfound hope that this was indeed possible, and as she adjusted her focus, Cherished decided to follow the stream of light to its origin. She found that the light was forging its way through a small opening in the back of the cavern. Cherished could feel her heart pound a little faster as she debated to herself, "Could this be the pathway leading out of my entrapment?"

With eagerness, she moved toward the opening and began grasping at the rock wall in search of loose rock.

Pathway **TO YOUR HEALING**

1. As Cherished embraced the truth concerning her identity and the love that was extended to her by the Spirit, her heart awakened more and more. She recalled the times of deep surrender to Life-Giver and she longed for that meeting place of unity with her Creator once again. The Spirit reminded her, "That meeting place is at the altar." He instructed her when she decided it was time to begin. Cherished placed on the altar all her burdens (the mental anguish and internal fears and pains), all her faults (ways she had judged or harmed herself or others) and the ways that she had ceased to follow after truth (Life-Giver's ways). Then, she invited Life-Giver to meet with her there.

    a. Jesus wants to meet you at the altar. Will you come to meet with Him there? It is a place of deeper surrender, but also deeper unity with Christ. He is waiting for you there.
    b. What burdens, pains, disappointments or fears do you need to place on the altar?
    c. What faults, judgments, failures or rebelliousness do you need to place on the altar?

2. Within that experience of repentance at the altar, Cherished found that Life-Giver had forgiven her faults. He not only

forgave her, but He gave *her* the power to forgive those who had harmed her and the power to forgive herself. This brought great freedom to Cherished. She was amazed to find that she felt lighter, and she was delighted that the light was penetrating the darkened cavern and the darkened places residing in her heart. Peace and contentment were replacing her pain and anguish.

    a. Will you open your heart to receive the forgiveness from your Savior, Jesus Christ? He wants to grant you freedom.
    b. Who (including others, yourself and God) do you need to forgive? Can you ask the Holy Spirit to empower you to do that? He is waiting to help you.
    c. Are you ready to ask the Holy Spirit to bring His light into those places and lift the weight of your burden?

3. Cherished noticed several things that had a grave impact on the enemy: (1) her heart as it was turned toward Life-Giver in trust; (2) her choice to find a way out of the darkness instead of giving herself over to it; (3) her renunciation of the lies that the enemy perpetrated. She recognized that as she changed her ways, her enemies did not have the same power over her. When she renounced her belief in the lies, their lies did not captivate her in the same way as when her mind was given over to the darkness. Cherished was beginning to understand that not only would the Spirit fight for her, but *she* held power over the enemy as well.

    a. Is there a turning of your heart that needs to happen? Is there a greater place of trust Jesus is calling you to? Write a letter to Jesus declaring your desire.
    b. Is there a part of you that is still embracing the darkness? What is the cause: hopelessness, shame, weariness, fear, or…?
    c. Is there a place in you where the Holy Spirit has already brought His freedom and light? Describe that place.

    d. Is there a lie of the enemy that you still believe? Can you, like Forsaken, begin to renounce the lie? What hold does the enemy have over you? Will you exercise your power?

4. As Cherished began to take in more *life* from the Spirit and gain freedom over her enemies, she desired to find a way out. She gained the renewed strength she needed to devise and execute a plan, and as she did so, she received hope and her burdens were lifted. She found that the Spirit was right there to guide her and empower her in her search.

    a. Are you able to receive *life* from the Spirit? In what ways is He extending Himself to you? What is your experience like?
    b. Do you desire a way out of the state you are in? Describe that.
    c. On the other hand, are you experiencing increased freedom and hope as you progress through the necessary steps to health? Describe that.
    d. In what ways are you noticing the Holy Spirit's guidance? Describe that.

5. Forsaken needed to believe again that she was Cherished. The Spirit revealed to her that Life-Giver's love never changed even in her disbelieving state. What had changed was her ability to recognize and receive His love. The other thing the Spirit revealed to her was that the *significance* Life-Giver had placed in her was still there. The enemy had lied to her and convinced her that there was nothing good left in her to save—that her significant worth was crushed or deadened through her life circumstances. The Spirit's revelation was one of awakening the life and vitality that was still inside her waiting to be revived.

    a. Was there a place in your journey where you believed that your life circumstances crushed and destroyed anything

good that was once present in you? Abuse and neglect can cause you to *feel* this is so. What was (is) this like for you?
b. What is the significance that the Lord Jesus has placed in you (gifts, abilities and goals)? What can you do to reclaim that significance?
c. The enemy sometimes progresses a step further and convinces us that the life of God that was originally placed in us was stolen and is no longer present. That is a lie. All Forsaken had to do was dare to trust again, and the Spirit began to awaken the life within her. What is your experience? What do you want to believe?

Chapter Seven

WALKING IN THE LIGHT

For you were once darkness, but now you are light in the Lord. Walk as children of light (Ephesians 5:8).

Cherished was determined to find an escape route from her dark prison. Fear and Shame tried many times to engage her in their schemes, but they failed. Finally they ceased their annoyances and relocated to the other side of the cavern.

Cherished continued her task of removing the stones that blocked her passage out. With each rock that she successfully dislodged, the tiny opening to the outside world expanded until a flood of light came pouring into her darkened cell. It had been so long since Cherished had experienced the light to this degree. She was amazed at its brilliance and how much it excited and strengthened her heart. Hope and faith, now emerging on their own from a wellspring of light deep within her, energized her further and created an ease to her forward movement. Even so, Cherished advanced cautiously, gradually adjusting her mind and heart to the projected *freedom*.

She was acutely aware that a part of her became invested in surging full speed ahead, crashing through all barriers and bearing her soul to the light. On the other hand, Cherished's mind challenged her with reservations about the seemingly enchanted place she was uncovering. Cherished was discovering that her mind and heart had grown so used to the repeated taunts of the enemy that, although she could now hear the voice of the Spirit, she needed to recultivate her behavior of turning toward Him.

As she continued her task of liberation—one dislocated stone after another—she reasoned within, "What will this new place be like?

Will my enemies be waiting to harass me further? Will I be strong enough to resist them and their lies this time? Will I find that my heart will deceive me once again or will I remember Life-Giver's truths?"

The Spirit, who had stationed Himself at her side and was assisting her in dismantling the wall, gladly responded to her.

"I will be with you," He said, "and I will teach you."

Cherished was hoping for some other detailed instruction from the Spirit, but as she reflected on His statement she determined, "*You* are all I ever need, Spirit."

Just then she remembered Life-Giver's words, "Where could I go from Your Spirit? Or where could I flee from Your presence? If I ascend up into heaven, You are there; if I make my bed in Sheol (the place of the dead), behold You are there… If I say, Surely the darkness shall cover me and the night shall be [the only] light about me, even the darkness hides nothing from You, but the night shines as the day; the darkness and the light are both alike to You" (Psalm 139:7–8, 11–12, AMP).

She thought, "Those words did not hold any meaning for me before, but I am thankful that they do now. There is nowhere that I can hide from the Spirit of Life-Giver. Even in the darkest cavern, He will bring His light." All the words Life-Giver had spoken to her through the years, as well as the truths from His Promise Book, were now streaming back into her consciousness, reviving her heart. She marveled at the way this was happening because she knew how energetically she and her enemies had worked at destroying them.

The Spirit reassured her, "Life-Giver's words are all here, Cherished, faithfully waiting for your desire to ignite them."

Cherished smiled broadly. It was the first sign of joy the Spirit noticed on Cherished's countenance since she left Life-Giver's kingdom. The Spirit's excitement overflowed Him as a deep, unrestrained holy laughter billowed up within Him and spilled out, exciting Cherished's heart as well. Cherished could not contain the exuberance she was now experiencing in her spirit. She could hear waves of holy laughter gushing through the caverns of her heart, bubbling up into the vast empty reservoirs in her soul, filling and refilling her and then bursting forth—flooding her grave-like existence with life.

This invasion of pure holy joy continued for a long time. Both Cherished and the Spirit were lost in this heavenly eruption until an eruption of a different sort gained their attention. It was the stirring sound of falling rocks that abruptly brought their focus back to the opening where they saw huge chunks of the cavern wall suddenly breaking free and cascading down around them. Amazed at the event and yet still attentive to this heavenly outburst of joy, Cherished was carried along in this stream of unrestrained celebration that was now evident in her surroundings as well.

In this electric atmosphere, the Spirit reminded her of something Life-Giver had spoken to her, "Child, if you don't praise Me, the rocks will cry out to Me!" (see Luke 19: 40). The Spirit continued, "I am teaching you something very valuable right now. I am teaching you that you *can* have joy in every circumstance because I am with you no matter what the circumstance. The joy that you are experiencing right now is only a taste of what I can give you. Let me fill you and My joy will be your strength and your reward."

Cherished's heart, now open to the truth that the Spirit was speaking to her, expanded further to this outpouring of joy. As joy flowed out, the walls that had entombed her continued to crumble until they came to rest at her feet. With haste the Spirit began to clear a path for her. To her astonishment, Cherished realized that this was the pathway to her much desired freedom, and in a voice larger than she had anticipated she shouted, "Thank You, Spirit! Thank You, Life-Giver! I'm ready to go wherever You want me to go."

Delighted, the Spirit scrambled to His feet and urged Cherished to take His hand for the remainder of the journey. He realized that her travels were not yet completed and she would still need His strength and companionship for the rest of her journey through the Valley of Despair. Even though her enemies had lost a great deal of their influence over her (due to her changed heart), the Spirit knew their stammering lies and their attempts to persuade her to turn back would not cease.

Before responding to the Spirit, though, Cherished was intent on gathering some *necessary* items to include with her. First of all, she secured her bag, examined its contents and, most importantly, noted that all of her original belongings were there. After everything was accounted for, she began searching the floor of the cavern in hopes of finding the shiny object that had initially shown her the way out. She didn't know exactly what she was looking for, so she asked the Spirit for help.

Eager to help her whenever He could, the Spirit skillfully extracted the small shiny object from the dirt that had temporarily encrusted it and placed it within her reach. When it was in her possession, Cherished gently brushed off the dirt and held it towards the light hoping to recapture some of the radiant colors. Dazzling color (satisfying her expectations) leaped across the surface of the stone and darted into the air. Once again Cherished was engaged by its fiery beauty and was reassured of Life-Giver's promise of *life*. Cherished stuffed the shiny stone into her bag as she reminded herself that there was one more *precious* stone that she wanted to take.

"I want a reminder of the altar I built and the way the Spirit met me here," she stated aloud, as she grasped a stone from the pile and added it to her belongings in the bag.

Thoughts of her upcoming liberation now captured her attention and her excitement built as she swiftly crawled through the newly excavated tunnel leading out of the cave. Her mind speculated on the whereabouts of her enemies, but Cherished soon discarded those thoughts as she entered the valley.

The first thing that pleasantly aroused her senses was the dense green foliage. It was inviting to her eyes and to her heart, and it seemed to welcome her into its midst. "Is this a part of the Valley of Despair?" she exclaimed to herself. "It is not at all like the other side of the valley. This feels strange, but it reminds me of the meandering gardens that wind their way around Life-Giver's home. The brightly colored flowers that border that path are not here; nonetheless, it is still very beautiful."

What was deceiving to most people who traveled this way, however, was that Enemy King still ruled over this land and his army remained active in this territory. Cherished was not yet aware of this, but the Spirit who had faithfully exited the cavern with Cherished was intent on teaching her that fact.

Without forethought, Cherished had started running headlong down the path when the Spirit aptly apprehended her. She had no idea that her enemies had returned for her and were waiting for her at the next turn of the path. Cherished knew the Spirit well enough to recognize that He always acted on her behalf; therefore, she willingly quieted her impetuous heart and yielded to His command.

Cherished noticed that a gradual change had taken place in her heart. Ever since the blockages had been removed, her heart had developed a greater desire to be submitted to the Spirit. With fondness in her voice, she remarked to the Spirit, "Thank You, precious Spirit, for helping me open the closed places in my heart so I can hear and *respond* to Your call." Cherished and the Spirit were both exceedingly happy that this was so, and they reveled in their mutual achievement.

As the Spirit moved close to her, Cherished observed a long, silvery object in His hand. When she realized it was a sword, she became alarmed. But before her mind could really grasp what was happening, the Spirit spoke, "This sword is for you, Cherished. I will teach you how to use it, but *you* must hold it in *your* hand. I will make you into a warrior like your leader, Life-Giver!"

Cherished was speechless. She questioned within herself, "How can I be a warrior, especially one like the grand Life-Giver, with all my failings and…"

The Spirit interrupted her thoughts by holding the large sword out to her and stating, "It is My power that is contained in the sword, not yours. But, it is your *will* that must wield it. Will you align your will with Mine and let Me empower you?"

Cherished was not sure she understood all of what the Spirit was asking her, but her heart was telling her, "Yes, yes, I want to be a warrior for Life-Giver! Make me His warrior."

The Spirit instructed her, "You must wield your sword in the face of your enemies and speak the words Life-Giver gives you. Do not fear. When you confront the enemy he will not see you, he will see Life-Giver, the One who goes before you."

As He spoke those words to Cherished, her spiritual eyes were opened and she reflected on the dream Life-Giver had given her (see chapter three). The battle between good and evil had been so vividly portrayed in that dream! She recognized that the evil army was powerful, but what she remembered the most were the hosts of warring angels ready to battle on her behalf.

"With that knowledge, I can be bold," she declared. And as she held out her hand to receive the sword from the Spirit, she added, "Teach me, Spirit, for I am Yours."

Pathway **TO YOUR HEALING**

1. As Cherished's heart turned toward Life-Giver, the Spirit strengthened her and new hope and faith entered her heart. She could now hear the Spirit encouraging her and she voiced her commitment to Him. Even though she questioned where the Spirit was leading her, she determined to trust Him and faithfully follow Him. Life-Giver's truths were now coming to her remembrance and she gladly embraced them, although she questioned her own ability to remember the truths and to resist the deception of the enemy.

    a. Prior to this time Cherished had become so disheartened that she had rejected the truth that once brought her so much life and hope. Now His truths were once again strengthening her heart and energizing her forward movement. In what way is the Word of God encouraging your forward movement? What specific promises have you been given?

    b. Cherished had desired detailed instructions from the Spirit to show her the way or let her know where she was going, but He simply told her, "I will be with you and I will teach you." (The Lord often does not give us the details we long for.) Her response to the Spirit was, "*You* are all I ever need, Spirit." Are you able to follow the Spirit even without specific directives? Can you tell Him that now?

    c. Cherished questioned her ability to hold on to the truth and resist the deception of the enemy. She knew that it would take time to cultivate that action again even though her heart had turned toward Life-Giver. What truth are you having difficulty believing for yourself? Can you let the Spirit help you?

2. Cherished learned that not only was the Spirit able to enter into that darkened place with her, He was also able to infuse her with joy. It was a joy that was available to her regardless of her circumstances and a joy that would come from deep within her spirit. This joy would not only bring her strength, it would also dismantle some of the walls that surrounded her. As the walls crumbled around Cherished, she was finally able to conceive of a way out and the Spirit cleared a pathway for her.

    a. Are you (or have you) experiencing the joy that comes to you by the Holy Spirit? What is (was) this experience like for you?
    b. How is this joy different from what the world brings?
    c. What internal blockage is (has) the joy dismantling? In what ways is the Holy Spirit clearing a path for you toward freedom?

3. When leaving the cave, Cherished decided to carry with her the objects that would remind her of the ways the Spirit had assisted her and the way her heart had submitted to Life-Giver. The Spirit helped her uncover the shiny object that had shown them the way out and she took a stone from the altar where she had submitted the hardened places in her heart to Life-Giver. It is good to have reminders of the times we meet with God.

    a. In what ways have you met with God? What can you take with you as a reminder of the way He has met you?
    b. In what way is the Holy Spirit leading you out of your confinement? Can you invite Him to be with you throughout the rest of your journey?
    c. What are the places you have yielded to Jesus?

4. As Cherished exited the cave, she was excited by her new surroundings and the realization that there was greater light and a more friendly landscape. She lost sight of the fact that this was still enemy territory and she needed to stay alert. Cherished

responded to the Spirit's prompting, however, and yielded to His command. She did notice that submitting to the Spirit was easier since the walls in her heart had been removed.

    a. In what ways have you lost sight of the fact that there is still enemy territory in your circumstances? How has that affected your behavior?
    b. What is the Holy Spirit commanding you to do?
    c. How easy or difficult is it to submit to the Spirit and why?

5. Cherished discovered that the Spirit was calling her to be a warrior. Much to her amazement He gave her a sword to use against the enemy. She had difficulty recognizing that she would have power like the warring angels she saw in her dream. But, the Spirit told her, "When you confront the enemy he will not see you, he will see Life-Giver." As Cherished received the sword she asked the Spirit to teach her.

    a. Are you ready to receive the call to be a warrior for Jesus? Why or why not?
    b. The Word of God declares, "Therefore submit to God. Resist the devil and he will flee from you" (James 4:7). As we submit to God and His ways the devil flees. In what area do you need to submit? Know that all your unrighteousness was nailed to the cross with Christ and that you are hidden in Him. You stand before the enemy clothed in Christ's righteousness.
    c. The power to resist the devil comes from the Holy Spirit. Pray for the Spirit's power.

Chapter Eight

THE PROMISE OF LIFE

Most assuredly, I say to you, he who hears My word and believes in Him who sent Me has everlasting life, and shall not come into judgment, but has passed from death into life (John 5:24).

Cherished stood tentatively at the edge of the pathway leading into the thick green brush on the east end of the Valley of Despair. The sword, which she gripped tightly in her hand, hung weighted at her side. The elation that had previously erupted within her, inciting her emancipation, had respectfully yielded to her growing solemn internal determination to answer the Spirit's call. "The rest of my journey will be directed by Life-Giver's Spirit," Cherished announced aloud. She wasn't sure whether her enemies were hiding in the brush within hearing distance, but in case they were, she wanted her intentions to be clear. Her heart was sure of one thing now, and that was to follow the Spirit wherever He would lead.

"I've made too many mistakes in the past," she muttered. "Now I will journey only with the Spirit!"

Witnessing her determination, the Spirit moved to her left side and took her arm. He thought, "She can raise the sword in her right hand and I will shield her left side—where her heart is."

Although Cherished couldn't see the Spirit beside her, she sensed His felt presence. "Spirit, please show me Your way," she requested.

The Spirit energetically responded and, together they started down the path. Cherished began to notice that her body felt considerably lighter than it had previously. Now she found it effortless to breathe despite the physical energy she was exerting. The spontaneous joy that she had experienced in the cave seemed to energize every cell in her body, immersing her senses in this marvelous interaction with *life*. She questioned how she had been so deceived by Death only just a short time ago and breathed a prayer that her heart would never return there. Cherished wondered if her enemies would be waiting to capture her again, but she vowed to stay alert and use the knowledge the Spirit had imparted to her throughout the rest of her journey.

She mused, "It is as if my eyes and ears are in two places at the same time. I can see this world right in front of me, but I also see another reality."

"That is correct," the Spirit replied. "This unseen world of the spirit will be revealed to you in greater measure as you give yourself to Me. Look there in front of you," He commanded her.

As Cherished stared out over the valley, she could see lush trees lining the far side of the valley and dense foliage that appeared to overflow the valley floor. She giggled as a gentle breeze brushed past her and moved out over the stilled branches causing them to twist and sway as if curtsying to greet a royal princess. Sparkling rays from the sun showered down on the valley, bathing the valley and Cherished's body in a warm glow. From this endearing place it was difficult for her to imagine her need for the sword that she still faithfully gripped in her hand.

She was ready to question the Spirit concerning it, when He anticipated her request and responded, "Look again, Cherished."

Cherished lifted her eyes towards the valley once again, and the spirit world became a reality. In the distance, rising above the rim of the valley—standing shoulder to shoulder—was Life-Giver's angelic army. "They are even more imposing than the ones I saw in my dream," Cherished remarked to herself.

These warring angels were dressed in full armor with golden breastplates that reflected the gallant sun as if combating the attacking rays. Their shields covered their bodies and bore the emblem of their King—a cross and a crown. And to Cherished's amazement, these mighty angels stood, set on task with swords drawn, ready for battle.

As Cherished looked out at these wondrous creatures, she noted that they stood a head taller than the trees they encircled. Then she looked down at her own small stature and questioned the Spirit, "How can I be effective against the enemy compared to this magnificent army?"

"Oh, child," the Spirit said, "*your* words hold a greater amount of power than *all* of the majestic army. It is *they* who are amazed at *you*."

When He spoke those words, another veil to the spirit world was lifted. Cherished began to hear groaning and weeping throughout the valley. It seemed as though the trees, shrubs, land and every living thing were crying out for life. A sea of broken and dying children appeared as far as she could see in every direction. Cherished began to weep and wail. Her cries poured from the very core of her being, out of the darkness, into the light of day as they were drawn up before the angelic army and into the heavenly realm.

Her weeping continued until she thought her heart would break, and from that broken place came Life-Giver's words, "This is the work you can enter into with Me, a broken heart for broken people; this is *My* heart, I will share it with you if you'll let Me."

Cherished could feel the weight of those words pressing deeply into her heart as she experienced the joining of her heart with the only One who can bring *life*, Life-Giver. As His heart merged into hers, her heart swelled with love for the brokenhearted. With her face in the dirt and the sword by her side, she wept and wept and wept. The Spirit, who had been silently observing her throughout this sacred event, was impressed with her yielded, compassionate heart. Wanting to impart to her a greater understanding, the Spirit moved close to her and placed His hand on her head. She soon found herself transported into a different realm:

There, in the presence of an array of angels and united with other faithful worshippers, she knelt on the massive white marble steps ascending to the throne of Life-Giver. With her head bowed and keenly aware that her heart was seeking the One who sat on the throne, she exclaimed, "How is it that I am here in such a holy place? You are the only worthy One, Life-Giver!"

Life-Giver answered her immediately. "I have called you here."

When He spoke those words, her heart was excited beyond measure and drawn more deeply into the divine union with her King. Not caring to move, she remained engaged in the sacred silence that embraced her and her King. The love that emanated from the Spirit and Life-Giver seemed to dwell over, around, and through everything—including herself—as she became caught up in this secret assembly.

Cherished looked down at an unfamiliar object that had been set in her hands (replacing the sword she had laid at her side) and in the hands of the many followers of Life-Giver. It was a golden bowl with something like sparkling stars flickering in and overflowing the bowl. Fascinated, Cherished looked around at all the beautiful golden bowls the others held; then her gaze came back to herself and she realized she was clothed in a stunning white garment. It was so unlike the garment of shame she had worn for so long. Her eyes were captivated by the brilliance of her new gown. "Thank you" hardly seemed sufficient for all Life-Giver had given her; however, speaking it from her heart, she said softly, "Thank You, Life-Giver."

Those words had barely escaped her lips when she heard shouts of praise coming from the hosts of angels and the followers. The throne room became immersed in adulation to the One who was able to change a garment of shame into a righteous gown. As she listened, the followers sang a song Cherished had never heard before. It captured more and more of her attention as it swirled around her head and summoned her heart. She noted it was a song of thanksgiving that only the followers sang—not the angels.

She asked, "Why is this so?"

One of the angels answered, "It is not our song to sing because it is a song of redemption."

Still kneeling before the throne, she now noticed a river (like the one in her dream) flowing out from Life-Giver, down from the throne and through those who knelt before the throne. It was as green as it was pure, and when she questioned why, Life-Giver replied, "The green represents My mercy." And as He declared this truth, the power of His mercy washed over her heart. All agony concerning its lost condition simply yielded to the One who could change it.

"I certainly have need of His mercy," she thought, as she surrendered more of her heart to Life-Giver.

From her prostrated position she heard a shout that echoed as if uttered throughout the entire heavenly realm, "He is merciful! Praise Him for His mercy. He is full of mercy, mercy, mercy!"

As Cherished remained in this splendid place and in the river coming from the throne, waves of mercy continued to wash over her. She entered into a timeless state where her single desire was to attend to this heavenly water drenching her soul. With each wave the sorrow and pain of the past was being washed away. The broken places in her heart were bathed in the waters of His mercy.

After awhile, she asked, "Life-Giver, what are You doing?"

He answered, "I'm healing you, child; I'm healing you," as fresh waves of His mercy came to cleanse her soul.

Cherished yielded more and more of her heart as the river of mercy flowed through her. She was at peace, but her experience was not yet complete. Her attention was now drawn to the bowl filled with sparkling stars. She asked Life-Giver, "What is it?"

In a voice thundering above the mightiest ocean roar, yet as tender as the cry of a mother for her young, He shouted, "It is the prayers of My people."

Simultaneous with His shout, the followers poured the contents of their bowls into the river. The river then began to expand and effervesce with life and strength as it parted the heavens and rushed to the earth below. Cherished peered over what seemed to be heaven's edge. She could see the mountains, valleys, and inhabitants becoming submerged in this bountiful life-giving river of mercy propelled by the prayers of Life-Giver's followers.

All of a sudden Cherished heard the blast of a trumpet and the hosts of angels declaring loudly, "Justice and mercy, justice and mercy, justice and mercy." The followers fell to their knees.

Cherished's heart paused in awe as a golden flaming chariot pulled by magnificent horses raced across the heavenly expanse towards the throne. The angels now joined the followers on their knees as King Life-Giver stood to His feet before them. Cherished, fixated on His immense majestic presence and the mountain of blazing fire transported in the chariot, watched as Life-Giver began seizing handfuls of fire and thrusting them into the river. He continued until the whole river was ablaze. The fire traveled wherever the river flowed.

The angels and followers cried out, "Holy, holy, holy is the One who sits on the throne. Judgment and mercy belong to Him. Purity and righteousness is in the life of the river."

Cherished felt so utterly unworthy, but strangely, at the same time, so sure that the One who stood before her held the power to make her holy and wholly His. Immersed in His river of justice and mercy, she understood what her journey was really about—a battle for her allegiance. "Life-Giver is the only One worthy of my heart," Cherished announced.

Cherished carefully placed the golden bowl on the marble stair she had knelt on. She cupped her hands and held her heart before Life-Giver. All heaven grew silent, yet all hearts were joined together as one, adoring their King.

King Life-Giver spoke into the silence, "Cherished, I am calling you. Are you ready to serve Me?"

"Yes, Life-Giver, I am ready," she replied.

"Then, come up here."

Fear and excitement weakened her. Nevertheless, her desire was to please Him, so she reached for the sword that remained beside her, somehow gathered herself to her feet and began the upward climb towards the throne. As she stood before Him, she was surprised and overjoyed at the sense of peace that she experienced in His presence. With head bowed, she stood quietly waiting His command.

Without a word, Life-Giver gently lifted her chin and raised her head. The moment their eyes met, a forceful, but inviting, holy love swept through her body. The magnetism of it drew her into Him as it excited her love for Him and renewed her resolve to follow Him.

Life-Giver now reached down and seized a handful of fire from the river. Turning towards her, He slowly and methodically touched the flame to Cherished's head, lips, heart and hands. He explained, "I am purifying what you think, speak, feel—what you hold in your heart—and do."

Instantly, her body became enflamed with this holy fire and she stood trembling as heaven echoed its cries, "Justice and mercy, justice and mercy, justice and mercy!"

"Oh, Life-Giver," Cherished blurted out, "who can live?"

"Cherished," He responded, "you never have to fear My justice as long as you remain in My mercy. Where My mercy river flows, My Spirit flows and He will never fail you."

King Life-Giver then took a broad step, removing Himself from her path, and with a grand gesture worthy of His title, drew His sword. The sudden clanging of the blade as it left the sheath resounded throughout the heavenly atmosphere. Cherished lifted her eyes and saw that the angelic army stood with weapons bared as well.

Cherished knew it was time for her to depart and answer Life-Giver's call. As she raised her sword, holy power surged through her arm and an enormous supernatural strength came into her. The river, this holy fiery river, was rushing in, rushing in, filling all the chambers of her heart with faith, faith, and more faith until she echoed the cry of the One who sent her:

"NOW, now is the time to go and answer His call!"

Cherished looked back over her shoulder at Life-Giver who nodded His agreement and approval at her. His eyes, now a dazzling fire, penetrated her eyes, piercing her soul and sealing it as His own. He explained, "Through your struggles the enemy wanted to capture your devotion, but I have kept you for My own. Do not fear. The One who has kept you will keep you. I will protect your heart as I send you to do My work."

Another trumpet sounded, and in the next moment Cherished was transported back to the Valley of Despair. This time, however, she was seeing with her renewed eyes.

Cherished was astonished to discover that even though her surroundings testified that she was, indeed, back in the valley from where she was plucked, she remained standing in the marvelous river that flowed from the throne. Above the far mountain ridge where the mountains meet the rim of the valley, she could see the river descending out of the heavenly realm, pouring down the mountainside and saturating the thirsty valley below. It delighted her that every living thing was exposed to the mercy coming from Life-Giver. With thanksgiving, her heart cried out, "mercy, mercy" as she watched the thirsty land drink the provision coming from heaven.

Then the holy fire began to pour from the heavenly realm until the river was fully ablaze. It was descending into the dark regions in the valley exposing the work of the enemy. Cherished viewed the chaos as the enemy army scattered seeking refuge behind fallen boulders, in trees and inside caves. She could see the ones who had held her captive: Abuse, Pain, Doubt, Death, Despair, Shame and Fear.

The Spirit instructed her, "Lift your sword, Cherished."

When she did, she could hear screeching coming from the enemy forces that had ensnared her and from the enemy dispersed in all parts of the valley, "No, why do *you* torment us? We know who sent you. Go away from us."

Emboldened by Life-Giver's presence in the holy fire, Cherished cried out, "Justice and mercy, justice and mercy, justice and mercy!" She began to travel through the valley, wielding her sword and successfully dispelling Enemy King's forces wherever she went.

Cherished came upon the valley floor and saw it was flooded with the broken, battered children the Spirit had shown her earlier. Her heart was gripped even more fiercely than it had been before. But as she began her petition to Life-Giver, she saw an incredible thing: first one child got healed, and then another, and then another! The children started smiling, then laughing, running, then jumping, up and down, up and down in the river. Cherished yielded to the excitement and began dancing in the river with them when the Spirit suddenly stopped her. "Cherished, this can only happen with your help," He said.

The Spirit reminded her of Life-Giver's words, "Will you go Cherished, will you go and take My healing to them?"

Cherished quieted her heart. She still felt so small and incapable compared to the task confronting her. Nonetheless, she recognized that her answer would have to rest in the only One who was able to bring it to pass. So she said, "Yes, yes I will go," and she said it again, "I will go. Yes, I want to go."

Each time Cherished said "Yes, I will go," her *yes* got louder and it gained force and it gained conviction. The Spirit attended her *yes* with *His yes* until all of heaven was in unison with her *yes*. The exciting thing to Cherished was that there was enough *yes* to bring it to pass—to bring the mercy river to the children and see them healed.

She couldn't hear or see Him right now, but Cherished knew that Life-Giver was pleased with her *yes*. And in her heart and mind, she could see Him smiling, smiling His wonderful, caring, loving, affirming smile—at her!

She paused for the embrace and then declared aloud, "I'm ready now, Spirit."

In response, the Spirit lovingly joined arms with her for the rest of their journey together. Cherished now knew that wherever she went, whatever she faced, she carried in her heart the healing presence of her beloved Life-Giver and the assurance of His faithfulness.

Pathway **TO YOUR HEALING**

1. Cherished gained a vision that there was something bigger than her immediate experience. Many times we get so focused on our own pain that we lose sight of the reality that there is a larger spiritual battle happening in the spirit realm. Cherished needed to give herself to the Spirit and His leading before her eyes were opened. Since her heart had been turned back toward Life-Giver she was in a position to *see* beyond her circumstances.

    a. Are you in a position to see beyond your circumstances? Why or why not?
    b. In what ways have you given yourself to the Holy Spirit's leading? Do you still need to profess that or change a heart attitude?
    c. In what ways have you been able to perceive the battle in the spiritual realm? (It does not have to come as a vision or dream. It can come as an understanding or knowledge to your heart or mind. There are many different ways that the Holy Spirit reveals spiritual truth to us. Don't limit the Holy Spirit.)

2. As Cherished's eyes were opened to the spiritual realm she gained a greater understanding of the forces behind her struggle. The Enemy King wanted her allegiance to be pledged to him so that she would renounce Life-Giver and His truths. The battle was really a battle for her heart—who would she give her heart to? Life-Giver explained to Cherished that He had kept her heart (even through her dark journey) and He was able to

continue to do so as she served Him. Cherished was strengthened by that revelation and she was able to answer His call.

    a. In what way (s) has Satan sought to capture your heart? When and how did you become aware of it?
    b. What was your response? Are you aware that Jesus is able to keep your heart? In what way (s) has He done that for you?
    c. Do you want to answer Jesus' call to serve Him?

3. Cherished was amazed at the power she held over the enemy that came from Life-Giver. She found that even the angels were amazed by her. As she learned how to speak Life-Giver's words and wield her sword, the enemies that had held her captive were now dispelled. In the vision Cherished also saw that the prayers of the people brought *life* to the river that flowed from Life-Giver's throne. Their prayers were important in spreading the healing waters to those that needed it.

    a. The Bible declares that the sword of the Spirit is the word of God (see Ephesians 6:17). What word of truth can you speak into your situation? What lie has held you captive that you need to dispel?
    b. Has the enemy convinced you that you are powerless? The Holy Spirit wants to infuse you with faith.
    c. Will you add your prayers to the river and bring healing to the brokenhearted?

4. Jesus calls each of us, as His followers, to be agents of His healing to a broken world. In our own wounded state we often wonder, "Why would He want to send me?" But as we open ourselves to His healing, we can in turn give it away. Our hearts can be softened to embrace His pain over the suffering of His people because we also have known that suffering and, beyond that, God's ability to heal. This is part of God's redemptive plan.

a. Where are you in the healing process? Have you opened your heart for Jesus to heal? Are some of your broken places receiving His mercy?
b. Jesus wants to share His heart with you for the broken-hearted. In what ways have you (have you not) experienced that? Are you open to that? Why or why not?
c. Sometimes it is in healing others that we are healed. Who can you pray with or intercede for this week?

5. Cherished decided to yield the rest of her journey to the Spirit and learn His ways. She was surprised to see the broken children in the river receiving healing and was excited by it until the Spirit reminded her that it could only happen with her help. Even though she still felt very small, she remembered Life-Giver's words, "Where My mercy river flows, My Spirit flows and He will never fail you." She remembered the supernatural strength that entered her as the holy fiery river filled her tiny being and enabled her to answer His call. She reminded herself that the same power that enabled her to answer the call would enable her to complete it. With renewed hope Cherished said, "Yes, I will go."

a. Have you experienced the strength that the mercy river of God can bring to you? Write about your experience.
b. Life-Giver touched Cherished's head, lips, heart and hands with the fire from His river. He explained, "I'm purifying what you think, speak, feel—hold in your heart—and do." In what area (s) do you need to be purified? Will you open that place to Jesus right now?
c. As a follower of Jesus Christ, what is the mission that He is calling you to? He *will* empower you. Can you answer, "Yes, I will go!"?

APPENDIX

GUIDELINES FOR GROUP STUDY AND PARTICIPATION

This book is designed to assist your healing process whether individually or as part of a group. I believe the most benefit is derived, however, in sharing your journey with others who are on the same path. The experience of abuse and its aftermath produces feelings of isolation, shame and unworthiness. These are best processed with others who have similar issues and with whom you can mutually find understanding and strength.

Therefore, if you are an individual in recovery picking up this book, I encourage you to hunt for at least one other individual who will be willing to walk through the process with you. If you are a pastor or leader picking up this book, I encourage you to begin a group. There are hurting people who need a safe place to process their pain. If that seems like a daunting task, some of the guidelines below can help you.

As leaders:

Create a safe environment—

- **Meeting place:**
    Creating a safe environment begins with finding a comfortable and quiet place to meet. Small rooms that accommo-

date each group are advantageous to a large meeting room, which facilitates several groups. Noise can be distracting and having other people in earshot can feel like a violation of confidentiality.

- **Boundaries:**

    Another way that you can establish safety in the environment is through recognizing the personal boundaries of each member and enforcing some group rules concerning them. Individual space is a key issue with abuse survivors. Chairs arranged in a circle are a must for group sharing, but be sure to ask the participants how close they prefer to be.

    An even more important issue of personal boundaries is the issue of touching. Most of the groups I have led have felt comfortable with the rule, "Don't touch another individual unless they ask." Discuss the options with the group and set the rules right from the beginning.

- **Respect:**

    Safety is also built through respect. As a leader you can promote respect in the group members through your respectful non-judgmental attitude. Speak from your adult and not from your authoritative self. Develop empathy by connecting with your own internal struggles. This creates a dynamic of joining with the member and not one of superiority.

- **Confidentiality:**

    Last, but in no way the least, are the rules involving anonymity and confidentiality. It is important that group membership not be revealed outside of group. This, admittedly, may be much more difficult in the church setting, but I believe it is vital to the health of the group that every effort be made to protect each individual. Another important rule is, "*whate*ver is shared in the group stays in the group." The only exception can be if someone threatens to injure himself/herself or another person. There must be foreknowledge of a plan to implement at those times.

Know your material—

- **Be prepared:**
  Do the work yourself throughout the week. Even if you have done it before, take it to a new level. Have a fresh experience to bring to the table as well as knowing the material inside and out.

- **Leader groups:**
  Ideally, leaders should have a time of going through the material for their own benefit with the involvement of sharing with other leaders. As you pursue healing for yourself, you will have more to give.

Group process—

- **Size:**
  Keep the groups small. Five or six is an ideal number. Try not to go over seven. You want to have time for everyone to share on the questions for that week.

- **Time:**
  Allow 60–90 minutes for the group process. I have found two hours is too long. Members tend to get weary because of the weight of the shared material.

  It is a good idea to time each individual's share. Three to five minutes usually works well with a wrap up warning at four minutes. If you don't time the shares, you open the door for someone to monopolize the meeting. Explain to the group that it is just a tool to insure that everyone will get a chance to share.

It is also important that no one interrupts the person sharing, even if the person pauses or is silent for a period of time. This kindness is a way of protecting the healing space.

- **Order:**

    My suggestion is that the leader begin by reading the explanation under #1, followed by reading question #a. The participant to the right (or left) will answer that part of the question. The leader can then ask, "Is there anyone else who would like to answer that question?" (Opening it up to the group makes room for the individual who has a burning desire to comment on that question.) After those shares, you can move on to part #b and the next participant and so on.

    Of course, it can be a much more complete study if every participant can comment on every question, but you have to consider the depth of the material and group size. If you decide to adopt that form, you may have to extend the study beyond the anticipated eight weeks.

- **Crosstalk:**

    Crosstalk happens when one person in the group comments on another person's share. In most twelve-step groups this is forbidden. One reason is that time can get away from you and questions do not get answered. The other problem with it is that individuals can fall into the trap of either trying to fix the other person or judge them.

    As an experienced therapist in working with groups, I like open sharing; but I know how to stop improper or unnecessary sharing. Leaders who are not familiar with group dynamics should not attempt this. Again, this can also lengthen the eight-week study.

    If you are going to enforce the "no crosstalk" rule, set it in the beginning and reinforce it during the group process. The later can be awkward sometimes, but a gentle reminder of the rule is all that is necessary. Try not to make a correction to what was spoken.

Summary—

Enjoy the process. I realize that might sound like a ridiculous statement given the seriousness of the issues; though, I find it exciting watching others (as well as myself) grow and gain freedom from the weight of the past and the hand of the enemy. We don't have to stay stuck. That is why I have put this book in your hands. I hope you find it a worthy part of your recovery.

ABOUT THE AUTHOR

Carol Romeo is a seasoned author, speaker, and marriage and family therapist. She has crafted five books throughout the past 2 decades of serving others with the accumulated wisdom that she gained throughout her personal recovery process and her experience counseling others. Carol received her bachelor's degree in psychology and her master's degree in marriage and family therapy from Azusa Pacific University. Carol feels passionate about her goal to bring wounded people to health and is convinced that it is vital to include spiritual training as part of the healing. This understanding moved her to gain a master's degree of practical ministry from Wagner Leadership Institute and functioned as a prayer counselor in numerous churches.

While thinking about how I want to present myself and my works to you, I was reminded by the Lord that the contents of my books are really a journey. First of all, they are **my** journey. Each book describes my struggles during that part of my life and how the Lord healed, delivered me and ushered me into a **new me**. This is a process whose stages are dictated by Christ and Him alone. It is a process designed for each of us individually because He alone knows our needs and what we need from Him to transform us into the **new whole** persons we were meant to be.

Books authored by Carol Romeo

Meditations from the River: Healing Waters for Troubled Times. Copyright 2008 by Carol Romeo. AuthorHouse Publishing, Bloomington, Indiana.

Traveling with the Life-Giver: A Spiritual Journey Through Recovery from Abuse. Copyright 2012 by Carol Romeo. AuthorHouse Publishing, Bloomington, Indiana.

Expect the Miraculous: A True Life Story of the Extraordinary Power of God. Copyright 2017 by Carol Romeo. WestBow Press, Bloomington, Indiana.

Be a Powerful Woman of God: A Testament of His Goodness. Copyright 2021 by Carol Romeo. Trilogy Christian Publishing, Tustin, California

Journey into Wholeness: Steps to Emotional Wholeness. Copyright 2022 by Carol Romeo. Brilliant Books, San Francisco, California

www.ingramcontent.com/pod-product-compliance
Lightning Source LLC
Chambersburg PA
CBHW060406080526
44583CB00012B/487